SECOND EDITION

LEGAL ISSUES and GUIDELINES

for Nurses Who Care for

 the Mentally Ill

LEGAL ISSUES and GUIDELINES

for Nurses Who Care for

 ## the Mentally Ill

Joyce Kemp Laben RN, MSN, JD, FAAN
Professor of Psychiatric Nursing
Vanderbilt University School of Nursing
Nashville, Tennessee

Colleen Powell MacLean JD
Attorney at Law
Nashville, Tennessee

National Health Publishing
A Division of Williams & Wilkins

Published by
National Health Publishing
99 Painters Mill Road
Owings Mills, Maryland 21117
(301) 363-6400

A Division of Williams & Wilkins

Printed in the United States of America
First Printing

Designer: Sandy Renovetz
Compositor: National Health Publishing
Printer: Edwards Brothers

ISBN: 1-55857-013-6
LC: 88-063448

To the loving memory of my father,
Berton John Kemp,
whose lifelong pursuit of learning
was an inspiration to his
children and grandchildren.

" 'Tis Education forms the common mind,
Just as the twig is bent, the tree's inclined."

—*A. Pope*

J.K.L.

and

James Arthur Sparks

"Kindness in words creates confidence.
Kindness in thinking creates profoundness.
Kindness in giving creates love."

—*Lao-tzu*

C.P.M.

PREFACE

The authors arrived at the decision to write a second edition of this monograph as a result of the feedback we received from nurses, attorneys, and nurse-attorneys who found the information to be helpful in their practices. Since the first edition was published, litigation in the mental health field has continued, especially in the areas of right to refuse treatment, commitment, and the duty to warn. We have updated the material where needed and have included an additional accounting of new laws, cases, and research.

Both authors have had extensive experience in working in state institutions as well as with community agencies. In these roles, Ms. Laben, as a psychiatric nurse and lawyer, and Ms. MacLean, as an administrator and lawyer, have observed the frustration and problems precipitated by the increased demands on mental health professionals to understand and respond to legal issues. This is particularly true for professionals who have received extensive education in their clinical specialties but little support or training in regard to the accompanying legal issues.

During the past 25 years the intervention of the legal system in mental health issues and subsequent litigation have resulted in more change in mental health facilities and programs than in the prior 200 years of our country's existence. Although these changes have occasionally been disruptive, and the cost of litigation is substantial, most professionals recognize that the ultimate result of the increased role of the legal system in setting standards for mental health care has, indeed, been to improve conditions, expand services, and increase the number and type of mental health professionals who provide these services. Therefore, it is well worth the time of all mental health professionals to become knowledgeable about the legal issues surrounding mental health, not only to protect themselves but also to protect the rights of patients and improve care through "preventive thinking."

After reviewing the massive number of cases and articles relating to mental health legal issues, we concluded that it would be an almost impossible task to summarize comprehensively the issues they raise. Therefore, it is not our objective to compile a catalogue of citations for cases and articles, but to provide an outline of basic concepts so that the professional can successfully identify pertinent legal issues in the situations they confront. Our goal is also to provide a useful resource for psychiatric-mental health nurses; however, *we are in no way attempting to provide a substitute for legal advice or a knowledge of specific state statutory and case law.* When they identify a legal issue involving their practice, professionals should not only utilize their own knowledge of the applicable state and federal law *but also seek legal advice.*

An additional objective is to point out and acknowledge the contradiction and misapplication of certain legal trends. For professionals who have recently entered the mental health field, these contradictions must be particularly confusing. For example, Thomas Szasz, a well-known psychiatrist and author, advocates the total abolition of involuntary commitment in order to prevent the intrusion of government into the lives of the mentally ill. However, no one has ever fully reviewed the possibility that the consequences of this action would be to force society to treat the mentally ill who refuse treatment as "criminals" when their behavior is dangerous, because no other option would exist. We must at least acknowledge that society will not tolerate certain behavior and will demand that some action be taken to isolate such individuals; if the option of civil commitment is abolished, the inevitable result will be the criminalization of the mentally ill who exhibit dangerous behavior.

Another illustration of conflicting legal concepts is the debate over the right to refuse treatment versus the right to

treatment in the least restrictive environment. Since the intro-
duction of pharmacotherapy, more individuals have been able
to function in the community rather than remain for long
periods in an institution. Recent cases that recognize the right
of an involuntarily committed patient to refuse treatment,
including medication, may result in the increased use of inpatient facilities and involuntary outpatient commitment because of patients' refusal to take medication and the subsequent exacerbation of their illness.

This book includes a discussion of the importance of adequate recording and reporting. Written communication of
treatments provided has long been an important aspect of
health care, but the practice of peer audit of nursing care to
evaluate professional performance is a relatively recent inno-
vation. Because of continuing litigation concerning care of the
mentally disabled and the requirement of audits by accrediting
organizations, mental health caregivers must realize that services provided to clients will be evaluated not only by an
employing organization but potentially by outside organizations such as government agencies and the judicial system.

Legal issues related to care of the mentally retarded are not
specifically discussed in this book, although many legal problems that concern this group also impact on the mentally ill.
These include such issues as rights in institutions, guardianship, and zoning for community group homes.

Although the content of this book is directed toward psychiatric nurses, other mental health professionals will find it
useful since they will be faced with the same legal issues in
clinical practice with clients in institutions and the community.

The authors would like to extend their gratitude to Melissa Paty, Marthagem Whitlock, and Ellen Pryor for their assistance and comments.

Encouragement from the faculty of the Department of Mental Health and Organizational Behavior at Vanderbilt University, especially that of Professor Carol Dashiff, Department Chair, is greatly appreciated. Tivis Nelson, Kathryn Ham, and Lois Kemp are thanked for their "pep talks" and support. Robert J. Laben is once again commended for his patience and tolerance during periods of inattention to him.

Special kudos to Janelle Gervickas, who never complained about retyping the manuscript and always conveyed that the content was interesting despite her repeated reading of the chapters.

We thank the staff of the Law, Medical Center, and Central Libraries at Vanderbilt University for assisting us in locating essential readings.

We continue to be indebted to those forensic patients who were detained for years without adequate health care or legal and judicial intervention and whose dilemma prompted us to begin our careers in forensic mental health. The plight of mentally ill offenders, especially those entangled in mental health and correctional systems that do not address their specific needs, continues to prod us to write about mental health law for our nursing colleagues in the belief that all of us together can improve the circumstances of this maligned group.

CHAPTER 1

Historical Trends

Laws governing the commitment and treatment of the mentally ill in the United States have been in force only within the last century. A historical view of social attitudes and responses to the mentally ill can help place the dramatic impact of recent legislation and litigation in proper perspective.

Although commitment to mental institutions was unknown until the early part of the last century,[1] the isolation of mentally and physically defective children on mountainsides and in pits is documented as early as 800 B.C. in Sparta.[2]

After the 1400s, beliefs in witchcraft became prevalent in Europe, and the colonists who came to America brought these beliefs with them. Persons were accused, convicted, and punished for witchcraft in the American colonies.[3] The practice of medicine had not evolved sufficiently to identify mental illness or to determine its cause or proper treatment.

During the reign of King Edward II of England, between 1255 and 1290, the *De praerogativa regis* was passed. This law established for the first time two classes of mentally disordered individuals: idiots and lunatics. The term "idiot" was used to refer to persons born without understanding; "lunatics," according to the law, were born with understanding but lost it later in life.[4]

The law gave the feudal overlord "the right to seize the lands of idiots in payment of the military service owed him by the mentally defective vassals."[5] Lunatics, on the other hand, might at some point in time recover from their illness and be

1

able to perform their duties to the overlord, and for this reason their lands could not be seized. A guardian, the king, was appointed through the Court of Chancery and had the power and prerogative to use the proceeds of the lunatics' properties for their support.[6]

Founded in London in 1247, the hospital of Saint Mary of Bethlehem was one of the first hospitals to provide for care of the mentally ill. It admitted lunatics beginning in the fifteenth century. Nicknamed "Bedlam," the hospital is reported to have used chains and irons in its treatment of mentally ill inmates.[7]

In colonial America, families cared for their own mentally ill members, and local tax money was available if a family was not able to provide adequately for the support of a mentally ill member.[8] Mentally ill persons who were indigent and without family care or support would often join a band of other indigents, who together would roam the country, living off the land. In America, prior to the mid-eighteenth century, many mentally ill individuals were "confined in local almshouses and jails and treated as common criminals and paupers."[9]

America's first institution to care for the mentally ill was the Pennsylvania Hospital in Philadelphia, established in 1752. In 1773, the first public mental hospital was opened at Williamsburg, Virginia, with a "keeper," rather than a doctor, in control of the institution.[10]

Benjamin Rush, considered the father of psychiatry in this country, in 1812 wrote the first publication about mental illness in America, briefly discussing the moral treatment begun by Philippe Pinel of France and William Tuke of England. The adherents of the moral treatment theory advocated treating the mentally ill with kindness and humanitarianism. Although he briefly presented moral treatment, the majority of Rush's treatise discussed bloodletting and "the use of the lash and of the chain and of the propriety of putting the patient in fear of death if the depleting methods already mentioned should not be effective."[11]

During the second quarter of the nineteenth century, there was a large immigration of various ethnic groups and a substantial increase in urban growth in the United States. These factors, coupled with economic depressions and the associated unemployment, led to increased numbers of mentally ill. These conditions induced the Secretary of State of New York to author a report which "fostered an increase in institutional care for dependent groups, with the care and treatment of the insane linked with welfare and dependence measures."[12]

In 1841, Dorothea Dix, while conducting a class of female convicts in West Cambridge jail in Massachusetts, discovered insane inmates living the prison. This discovery led her to examine almshouses and jails and hospitals for the mentally ill. She found conditions in these institutions so deplorable that she devoted considerable time to traveling across the country encouraging state legislatures to build hospitals to house and care for the nation's mentally ill.

Throughout her travels, Dix advocated moral and humanitarian treatment of the mentally ill, and the construction of institutions to house them. Despite her strenuous efforts, however, the mentally ill frequently were sent to asylums without adequate planning for their care, and the moral treatment she favored was not effectively continued.[13] Although she did make some progress, many of the hospitals were located in isolated rural areas, breaking the patient's ties with their families. Such separation is now recognized as detrimental to the treatment of the mentally ill.

Care and treatment reached a turning point in America in the 1860s, owing to the experience of an Illinois woman, Mrs. E.P.W. Packard. Reportedly sane, Mrs. Packard was committed to the Illinois State Hospital by her husband under an 1851 state commitment law that allowed a man to commit his wife to an institution, virtually without cause.

Mrs. Packard published several reports of her experience and treatment in the hospital. Upon her release, she devoted considerable time and money in an effort to alter the law. Not unlike Dorothea Dix, Mrs. Packard traveled extensively for several years, addressing state legislatures and campaigning to change state commitment laws. In several states she was successful, and laws were altered to provide such procedural safeguards as notice of commitment and trial by jury to determine insanity.[14]

During the 1870s, many states passed legislation that included safeguards preventing the commitment of sane individuals. The guidelines for the legislation were patterned after the safeguards inherent in criminal law. In some states, a jury was impaneled to decide the mental status of the individual. In spite of the apparent progressiveness of these laws, those persons judged mentally ill could be committed for indefinite periods of time, and upon commitment they relinquished all civil rights.[15] The perception of mental illness and the commitment process were "for the most part perceived in human rather than strictly legal terms."[16]

In 1872 Iowa passed a law permitting patients letter-writing privileges. Other states, including Pennsylvania and Massachusetts, followed suit. Hospital superintendents viewed this change as an assault on their professional judgment and autonomy and an interference with the doctor-patient relationship.[17]

In 1890, New York passed the State Care Act, which divided the state into districts, each with a state hospital responsible for caring for the district's own mentally ill patients. Supervision of the care of these individuals was coordinated by the State Commission on Lunacy, whose name was later changed to the State Department of Mental Hygiene.[18] The name change was significant because it reflected a modification in attitudes toward treatment of the mentally ill.

By the end of the nineteenth century many hospitals for the mentally ill had been constructed, and care and treatment were primarily under the control of the state system.[19] The work of the pioneers in the field had demonstrated the need for an organized, sanctioned method of dealing with the problem of growing numbers of mentally ill people, and state hospital systems were the result. Care of the mentally ill remained materially unchanged until the latter part of this century. The mental health system, under the direction of state governments, functioned within rigid confines until after World War II.

As expertise in the field of psychiatry developed, psychiatrists maintained that laws modeled after criminal law were not satisfactory. Psychiatrists throughout the United States began to criticize the commitment laws, which overlooked advances that had been made in psychiatry, and began advocating less formal judicial proceedings in favor of admission based on medical and psychiatric opinion. It was their position that the inclusion of psychiatrists in the admissions process reduced the likelihood that wrongful commitments would take place, and that protection procedures were no longer necessary.

In 1952, the National Institute of Mental Health published a document entitled the Draft Act Governing Hospitalization of the Mentally Ill. This publication, in an effort to ease and broaden patients' access to hospitals and the treatment they provided, advocated voluntary admissions based on certifications by physicians, as well as more formal procedures when indefinite commitment was necessary. The Draft Act Governing Hospitalization not only placed emphasis on primary treatment of the mentally ill, but sought to virtually remove judicial intervention from the admission process by advocating notice of a hearing and jury trial after admission, rather than before.

Largely as a result of criticism by psychiatrists and the actions of the National Institute of Mental Health, many states adopted the procedures that had been advocated. Medical, rather than judicial, certification became more prevalent. As the movement grew, however, so too did the potential for abuse of due process procedures for mentally ill individuals.

In the 1960s, the New York Bar Association conducted a study which concluded that only 10% of the patients committed in New York actually had a hearing, and that patients usually did not receive notice of the hearing.[20] In 1961, the Joint Commission on Mental Illness and Health published a report stating that the institutional system of mental health care in this country had been a "dismal" failure.[21] The report led to the passage of the Community Mental Health Centers Act of 1963, which authorized monies for the construction of comprehensive centers to be completed over a period of years. As the comprehensive centers were built, the populations in state mental hospitals did decrease. Despite lower hospital populations, however, not everyone was satisfied with hospital treatment of the mentally ill.

Just as the pendulum had swung in favor of the intervention of physicians in the early 1960s, the movement was reversed in the early 1970s when activist lawyers began filing cases based on patients' rights and the right to treatment while hospitalized. The explosion of lawsuits filed to improve mental health care continues into the 1980s, and there has been a growing trend toward suits based on the patient's right to refuse treatment. Many of these suits were filed in federal courts, as state laws were restrictive and outdated. Numerous state laws have now been updated and revised to conform with rulings of the federal courts.[22] Implementation of court orders, however, can take years. The famous right-to-treatment suit *Wyatt v. Stickney*, filed in the state of Alabama, went through a "15 year odyssey of legal and political maneuvering" before it was finally settled.[23]

Many of the abuses in state hospitals have been alleviated through the discharge of large numbers of patients, increased funding to improve the quality of care available in state hospitals, and the employment of professional instead of lay personnel. With the discharge of patients from mental hospitals, another problem has emerged. Large numbers of ex-patients have been dismissed from the protective environment offered by hospitals and institutions and are wandering the streets without adequate aftercare. In recent years, ongoing care and treatment in inpatient and community settings have become relatively common; however, community mental health centers were never able to fulfill the expectations of curing or maintaining the chronically mentally ill individual within the community.

A recent publication points out that our national mental health policy supposedly advocates outpatient care with deinstitutionalization. However, data indicate that inpatient episodes number 3 million, or "about sixty percent more than that typically reported in the literature."[24] Currently most admissions for psychiatric problems are to general hospitals that do not have separate psychiatric units.[25] Whether the legal rights of these individuals are being protected has not been explored.

In New York City a policy of involuntarily detaining individuals who may be a danger to themselves in the foreseeable future has been undertaken. There is some question as to whether removing the "immediate danger" requirement for commitment without changing the law is valid.[26]

Another trend is the presence in the mental health system of patients' rights advocates. The state of Maryland in a 1985 consent decree "agreed to the establishment of both an internal grievance system and a legal advocacy system."[27]

Trends in the mental health field have changed dramatically in the past 100 years. The problems of treatment of the mentally ill have created their own concerned experts in the mental health and legal professions. Each profession has its own particular concern for the plight of the mentally ill, and each has contributed to advances in the field.

Although nurses have been employed in mental health facilities for years, only recently have nurses with specialized education been using this knowledge to make an impact on mental health care. With the formation of specialty groups in psychiatric nursing and the nurse-lawyer association, it is anticipated that nurses, as a group, will voice their concerns with increasing frequency.

Since mental health laws vary widely from state to state, it is important for nurses in each state to maintain lines of communication and support in advocating the rights of patients.

References

1. Richard B. Saphire: The Civilly-Committed Public Mental Patient and the Right to Aftercare. *Florida State University Law Review*, 4, 1976, pp. 232–295, at 238.
2. Marcia P. Burgdorf and Robert Burgdorf, Jr.: A History of Unequal Treatment: The Qualifications of Handicapped Persons as a "Suspect Class" Under the Equal Protection Clause. *Santa Clara Lawyer*, 15, 1975, pp. 855–910, at 833.
3. John Biggs, Jr.: *The Guilty Mind*, New York, Harcourt, Brace and Co., 1955, p. 62.
4. S. Sheldon Glueck: *Mental Disorder and the Criminal Law*, Boston, Kraus Reprint Corp., 1925, p. 128. Holly Wilson and Carol R. Kneisl: Forensic Considerations in Psychiatric Nursing. In *Psychiatric Nursing*, Menlo Park, Cal., Addison-Wesley Publishing Co., 1979, p. 723.
5. Glueck: *Mental Disorder*, p. 125.
6. Ibid., p. 126.
7. Wilson and Kneisl: Forensic Considerations, p. 723.
8. Saphire: The Civilly Committed Public Mental Patient, p. 239.
9. Ibid.
10. Richard Allen, Elyce Ferster Zenoff and Jesse Rubin: *Readings in Law and Psychiatry*, rev. ed., Baltimore, The Johns Hopkins University Press, 1975, pp. 6, 7.
11. Ibid. p. 6.
12. Wilson and Kneisl: Forensic Considerations, p. 726.
13. Ibid.
14. Ibid. p. 728.
15. Ibid.

16. Gerald Grob: *Mental Illness and American Society, 1875–1900*, Princeton, N.J., Princeton University, 1983, p. 11.
17. Ibid., p. 48.
18. Wilson and Kneisl: Forensic Considerations, p. 729.
19. Norman Dain: The Chronic Mental Patient in 19th Century America. *Psychiatric Annals*, 10, no. 9, September 1980, p. 19.
20. Wilson and Kneisl: Forensic Considerations, p. 720.
21. Ibid., p. 729.
22. Leonard Rubenstein and Jane Yohalem: The Courts and Psychiatric Disability. In Arthur Meyerson and Theodora Fine (eds.): *Psychiatric Disability: Clinical, Legal and Administrative Dimensions*, Washington, D.C., American Psychiatric Press, 1987, p. 440.
23. John Parry: 1987 in Review. *Mental and Physical Disability Law Reporter*, 12, no. 1, 1988, p. 8.
24. Charles Kiesler and Amy E. Sibulkin: *Mental Hospitalization: Myths and Facts about a National Crisis*, Newbury Park, Cal., Sage Publications, 1987, p. 272.
25. Ibid.
26. Mary Wylie: Reinstitutionalization in New York. *The Family Therapy Networker*, November-December 1987, pp. 30, 39.
27. Paul Appelbaum: The Rising Tide of Patients Rights Advocacy. *Hospital and Community Psychiatry*, 37, no. 1, January 1986, pp. 9–10.

CHAPTER 2

Basic Issues in the Provision of Mental Health Services

Confidentiality and Privilege

Understanding the issues of confidentiality and privilege is imperative when providing therapeutic care for patients or clients.* Confidentiality is the legal and ethical responsibility to keep all information concerning patients and clients private; nurses as well as other health professionals must not divulge or release information given or available to them as part of their professional duties to persons not properly authorized access to that information.

Privilege is a narrower concept than confidentiality. It is created by statute to protect information elicited from clients and is granted only to specified professionals to ensure that the information will be kept private and confidential unless the client permits release. Specifically, privilege means that the stated professional cannot release any information received from clients without their authorization. Such privilege has been traditionally granted through statutes to lawyers, clergy, and physicians. With the expansion of mental health services,

---

* In this book the term "patient" is used for persons treated in an inpatient setting; "client" is used for individuals treated in the community.

11

other professionals such as psychologists and social workers have been also granted privilege in some states.

Privilege belongs to the client and can only be asserted by the client; it does not exist unless some kind of professional, therapeutic relationship exists.[1] Privilege pertains only to information obtained during the therapeutic relationship where there are no third-party witnesses. The patient or client has the right to waive the privilege and ask that information be given to a requesting source. One state, however, has allowed an exception to this rule: Illinois allows a psychiatrist the right to refuse to release information despite a patient's waiver, in the interest of the patient.[2]

Confidentiality is a broad concept governed by state statutes and professional ethical codes, which prohibits all professionals involved in the provision of mental health care from releasing information about specific clients unless requested to do so by the client or otherwise permitted by law. Almost every state has a specific statute governing confidentiality and the manner in which information can be released. This is a statute with which all nurses should be familiar.

In recent years, patients and clients have lost some of their control over the dissemination of private health information to insurance companies, health care facilities, employers, and the government.[3] In addition, secretaries, billing clerks, and other personnel may have access to an individual's record. All staff who have access to this information should be trained to avoid unnecessary revelations concerning a client's health care status. Health professionals have been observed discussing patient care on elevators, in halls, and in radiology departments in close proximity to other patients and visitors.

A minority of states have privilege provisions covering nurses.[4] Two client cases involving nurses and the issue of privilege were *State v. Sweet* and *Myers v. State*.

In *State v. Sweet*, a Vermont case, a defendant (Mr.Sweet) was brought into an emergency room by the state police after a motorcycle accident.[5] The nurse asked Mr. Sweet to sign a consent-to-treatment form. He stated to the nurse that he was too drunk to sign the form, but he subsequently complied. He was later convicted of driving while under the influence of intoxicating liquor and appealed on the issue of whether the nurse's testimony regarding his comments about being drunk could be admitted into evidence. The Vermont patient privilege statute reads as follows:

> Unless the patient waives the privilege or unless the privilege is waived by an express provision of law, a person authorized to practice medicine or dentistry, a registered professional or licensed practical nurse...shall not be allowed to disclose any information which [she] acquired in attending a patient in a professional capacity, and which was necessary to enable [her] to act in that capacity.[6]

The court decided that the information was admissible on the basis of the nurse's testimony that the defendant's statement was not necessary for her to act in her professional capacity. The court further declared that the nurse was fulfilling not a professional duty but a clerical duty required for all incoming patients except those in critical condition. One might challenge the accuracy of this nurse's testimony on the basis that professional nurses begin to assess an individual in an emergency room the minute the interview commences.

In *Myers v. State*, a female defendant, who was later convicted of murder, ingested an overdose of tranquilizers at the time that she killed the victim.[7] On admission to the mental health unit of the hospital after her physical condition had stabilized, she was interviewed by a nurse who was eliciting information for a questionnaire developed by the mental health nursing staff. The defendant was asked, "How do you feel about being on the unit?" The defendant replied, "I have failed and I will have to face the music." The defendant objected to this statement being introduced as evidence at the trial. The state of Georgia has no specific statute providing privileged communication for nurses. Since the nurse was not working under a psychiatrist at this particular time, the court decided that statutory privilege did not extend to her. If there had been a state law including nurses under the privilege doctrine, the nurse probably would not have been allowed to testify. If the defendant had stated the same words to a psychiatrist, in all likelihood the statement would not have been admissible.

There is some question as to whether privilege extends to participants in group therapy, which is an effective mode of treatment for many individuals with specific behavioral difficulties such as sexual addiction or a repeated pattern of antisocial behavior. The freedom to disclose very personal information is imperative in order to engage other members of the group to act as therapeutic agents and to form a trusting relationship. The only reported case to date on this subject has upheld the concept that communications within this setting are privileged.[8]

There is some concern about whether privilege extends to persons working under the supervision of a protected professional. Some cases uphold the privilege for the supervised person and others do not. Several of the adjudications were based on whether the supervisor had an actual professional relationship with the patient.[9]

When working with patients and clients in a psychiatric setting, it is important to be aware that a patient may not want anyone to know that mental health care is being provided. Secrecy is a primary concern of many patients. Slovenko points out that "treatment of mental disorders is more clandestine than treatment of physical disorders."[10] If one calls a general hospital to inquire about a patient, the operator is free to acknowledge that the person is hospitalized. However, this is generally not the case when inquiries are made about a patient in a psychiatric hospital. Acknowledgment of the person's presence in the facility is usually prohibited by the state statutory provisions regarding confidentiality.

Release of Information

Before information is released to another agency, proper authorization must ordinarily be provided. Professionals should never release information based on a telephone inquiry unless they can determine that the person has a right to the information and they can confirm the identity of the inquirer. The most common method of authorization is a release form signed by the client. The form should include certain elements, such as precisely what information can be released, to whom, and for what period of time.[11] In addition, most state confidentiality statutes authorize the release of information pursuant to a court order even if the client objects. If the state statute authorizes release only by a court order, a subpoena, which can be issued unilaterally by an attorney, does not provide proper legal authority for release. However, it is imperative that the professional respond to the subpoena by requesting that it be quashed or that a court order be issued.

Dissemination of information that may be legally released under the confidentiality statute may be prohibited if the information was obtained through a privileged relationship. If the client does not authorize release of privileged information, the professional may have to refuse to provide such data, even if a court order is issued. Such a dilemma would require the professional to go through a court hearing to resolve the question.

Halleck specifies situations in which a professional would be obligated to report confidential information without the regularly required release or court order. For example, if a physician had as a patient an airline pilot whom he knew was abusing alcohol or drugs, this information would have to be reported to the physician for the airline involved, on the basis of the doctrine of obligation to the welfare of others.[12] Another exception is when the client's acts or utterances may threaten a third party. This exception is discussed later in this chapter.

Access to Records

Courts have generally assumed that the medical record of a hospital or clinic belongs to the health care facility, and that the information therein belongs to the patient or client.[13] Some states have laws mandating a person's access to his or her own records, but even in those states it may be difficult for the person to obtain the record unless it is released to a physician or an attorney.[14] Halleck comments that there is a good case for allowing nonpsychiatric patients right of access to their records. He has some reservations about allowing a psychiatric patient to examine his own record, especially if the patient is acutely disturbed. According to Halleck, the patient could misinterpret the data or could be frightened by the contents.[15]

Stein and associates studied the effects of patient access to records on staff and patients in a psychiatric unit of a community general hospital. Patients reported that they felt better informed, and the staff said that they contemplated more extensively what they wrote in the records. Availability of staff to discuss the contents of the record seemed important to the success of the program.[16]

Duty to Warn Third Parties

An additional exception to confidentiality and privilege has developed as a result of a landmark decision in California, *Tarasoff v. Regents of the University of California*.[17] A young man, Prosenjit Poddar, was being treated by a psychologist at the University of California. He communicated to the therapist his intention of killing a young woman who was in Brazil at the time of the threat. The psychologist called campus security, who talked with Mr. Poddar but determined that he did not need to be detained. There were no further therapeutic interventions by the psychologist.

Mr. Poddar came from the *harijan* ("untouchable") caste in India and enrolled at the University of California at Berkeley as a graduate student in 1967.[18] He met Miss Tatiana (Tanya) Tarasoff in the fall of 1968. They saw each other weekly during that semester, but Mr. Poddar misinterpreted a kiss on New Year's Eve to indicate that there was a serious relationship. When he expressed his feelings toward her, she communicated to him that she saw other men and was not interested in an intimate relationship with him. With this rejection, he became depressed and neglected his studies, health, and physical appearance. During the summer of 1969, at the encouragement of a friend, he sought psychological counseling. During this time, Miss Tarasoff was spending the summer in South America. When she returned, Mr. Poddar stopped his sessions with the psychologist who warned the campus police. The following event then occurred:

> On October 27, 1969, defendant went to Tanya's home to speak with her. She was not at home, and her mother told him to leave. The defendant returned later, armed with a pellet gun and a kitchen knife, and found Tanya alone. She refused to speak with him, and when he persisted, she screamed. At this point the defendant shot her with the pellet gun. She ran from the house, was pursued, caught and repeatedly and fatally stabbed by the defendant. He then returned to Tanya's home and called the police.[19]

Mr. Poddar was later convicted of second-degree murder, but that conviction was overturned on appeal for improper jury instruction. Mr. Poddar returned home to India.

Mills et al. write that the therapist recognized the threat of violence but called the campus police instead of the city police. At the time, a new mental health civil commitment act had been in effect in California for only two months. According to Mills et al., "The *Tarasoff* case actually involved not a failure to recognize and act on potential violence, but a failure to use the appropriate social-legal interventions as therapeutic modalities."[20]

The family brought suit against the University of California. The Supreme Court of California ruled that when a therapist determines that an individual presents a danger to another individual, there is a duty to warn the intended victim. In such an instance, the confidential relationship must cease, because "the protective privilege ends where the public peril begins."[21] Since this decision, 12 states and several federal jurisdictions have found a duty to protect third parties.[22] Beck evaluated the cases that have been decided and classified them into three categories: clearly foreseeable victims, questionably foreseeable victims, and unforeseeable victims. This format will be used to analyze some of the cases.

Clearly Foreseeable Victims

In *McIntosh v. Milano*, a New Jersey case, Dr. Milano was treating an adolescent boy who had been involved with drugs. The boy had fantasies about a young woman (Miss McIntosh) who lived next door and expressed some jealousy toward her, which he communicated to the therapist. He had possessive feelings toward the young lady and was "overwhelmed" by the relationship. There was evidence that the adolescent had fired a BB gun at either Miss McIntosh's or her boyfriend's car and at the windows in the McIntosh home. He also carried a knife and showed the weapon to Dr. Milano. The boy later murdered the young woman, and a wrongful death action was brought by the deceased woman's mother against the psychiatrist for his failure to warn the intended victim. An expert witness for the plaintiff testified that the youth was a dangerous individual and that the object of his aggression was Miss McIntosh. The court noted that although confidentiality is important, it is not the only consideration. The welfare of the individual and the community must come first, particularly if the duty to disclose is compelled by law, or if an imminent danger to the patient or society exists.[23] This case has troubled many professionals because there was no actual threat to a specific person. Kermani and Drob write, "Unlike in Tarasoff where the main question was whether the therapist should violate confidentiality to report a threat, the issue in McIntosh becomes the therapist's duty to predict and warn about impending violence."[24]

In another case, John Peck, 29 years old, was an outpatient of the Counseling Service of Addison County, Vermont, in treatment with a counselor-psychotherapist. He and his father had an argument which resulted in Mr. Peck packing a suitcase and leaving home. He went to the Counseling Service and explained to his therapist that he was angry with his father. The therapist negotiated with Mr. Peck's grandparents for him to stay with them. The following day he discussed his anger with his father in a therapy session. Five days later he stated to the therapist that he wanted to "get back at his father," and could do this by burning down his father's barn. The therapist elicited a verbal promise from Mr. Peck not to burn down the barn. This matter was not discussed with any other staff members.

Shortly thereafter Mr. Peck did burn down his parents' barn. The parents brought suit against the therapist to recover damages for their property loss, which they asserted resulted from the therapist's negligence. The lower court dismissed the action following the trial, and the parents appealed. The appeals court ruled the following:

The mental health agency, by and through its counselor-psycho–therapist, had a duty to disclose to the parents that the outpatient had threatened to burn down the barn. The failure of the mental health agency to disclose to the parents the outpatient's threat to burn down the barn constituted breach of duty owed by the mental health agency to the parents.[25]

The evidence supported a finding that the parents were 50% comparatively negligent in causing their barn and its contents to be destroyed. Stone writes that this decision imposes the same standard of reporting on all mental health professionals and imposes not only liability for harm to third parties but liability for property damage as well.[26]

Questionably Foreseeable Victims

In 1980 a decision was rendered by the California Supreme Court that has been labeled shocking.[27] In *Thompson v. County of Alameda*, a young man, James, was released from an institution to the custody of his mother. James had indicated that, if released, he would kill an unidentified child in his neighborhood. Within 24 hours of James' release, he assaulted and murdered the plaintiff's son, who was 5 years of age. The victim's parents brought a lawsuit for wrongful death.

The court ruled that, because there was no specific identifiable victim, no duty existed to protect the youngster. The court also relied on a public policy consideration that would allow public officials to release prisoners, juvenile offenders, and patients without assuming risk of liability for mistakes.[28]

In a Maryland case, *Shaw v. Glickman*, a lawsuit was brought against a psychiatrist (deceased), a psychiatric nurse, and a psychologist. A couple experiencing marital problems was in group therapy. The wife had an affair with another member of the group, a dentist; the husband, finding the wife in bed with him, shot the dentist but did not kill him.

A suit was brought against the team, who knew of the liaison, for failure to warn the dentist of the potential danger. The judge ruled in favor of the defendants on the basis of the confidentiality of the psychiatrist-psychologist-patient relationship. The decision stated, "The lips of the psychiatrist or psychologist have been statutorily sealed shut subject to being unsealed by the patient or the patient's authorized representative."[29] In addition, the patient had never threatened the victim.

Unforeseeable Victims

In a Nebraska decision in the case of *Lipari v. Sears, Roebuck & Co.*, Ulysses L. Criff had been hospitalized at a Veterans Administration Hospital for psychiatric care. While participating in a day care program, he purchased a gun. He later withdrew from the program, against medical advice. Approximately six weeks later, he entered a restaurant and fired shots into a crowded dining room, killing Dennis Lipari and blinding his wife. The estate of the deceased brought suit against the store that sold the gun; the store subsequently brought the government into the suit to indemnify and contribute to any damages awarded to the plaintiff. The negligence law of the state of Nebraska was applied:

> To summarize, this Court is of the opinion that under Nebraska law the relationship between a psychotherapist and his patient gives rise to an affirmative duty for the benefit of third persons. This duty requires that the therapist initiate whatever precautions are reasonably necessary to protect potential victims of this patient. This duty arises only when in accordance with the standards of his profession, the therapist knows or should know that his patient's dangerous propensities present an unreasonable risk of harm to others.[30]

The court commented that, even when a psychotherapist makes an error in judgment, that behavior is not in itself basis for finding the professional negligent. The currently preferred mode of treatment is the least restrictive alternative. The court stated that the plaintiff must prove that the VA employees could have foreseen an unreasonable risk to the Liparis (or someone of that class of persons) and failed to act to civilly commit Criff. The defendants settled this case for $200,000, and the matter was never brought to trial.[31]

This case has caused concern because there was no identifiable victim prior to the shooting. Beck stated that, "Only two courts have held that such a duty applies while seven have indicated that it might; twelve courts have held on various grounds that it does not.[32]

In *Petersen v. State*, Larry Knox was on probation for second-degree burglary.[33] The terms of his probation included participation in mental health counseling and abstention from controlled substances. On April 16, 1977, Mr. Knox cut out his left testicle with a knife. His brother found him and took him to a U.S. Army hospital for treatment. Because Mr. Knox exhibited delusional beliefs and hallucinated, he was evaluated by a mental health professional and admitted to a state hospital for 72 hours. The physician, Dr. Miller, knew of the burglary conviction but was not aware of the conditions of the probation. Mr. Knox told Dr. Miller that he frequently used drugs and had used "angel dust" prior to cutting himself.

On April 22, 1977, an extension of Mr. Knox's commitment was requested and was granted by the Superior Court. On May 8, 1977, after returning from a pass, he was stopped by the hospital security personnel for reckless driving on the grounds and maneuvering his car in circles. The following morning he was discharged. The opinion of the physician was that Mr. Knox was not schizophrenic but had had a schizophrenic-like reaction from the angel dust. He was assessed to be in full contact with reality.

Five days later, Mr. Knox drove through a red light at 50 to 60 miles an hour and hit the plaintiff. Witnesses reported that he appeared to be under the influence of drugs. An action for negligence was instituted against the state. Two years after this incident Mr. Knox raped a woman and murdered both her parents.[34] Testimony was admitted in *Petersen* from two psychiatrists who had examined Mr. Knox and diagnosed him as having paranoid schizophrenia.

The court held that the psychiatrist should have committed the patient or taken some action to protect the public. The plaintiff was awarded $250,000. Again this decision caused consternation as no specific potential victim could be identified before the incident occurred.

Professional Practice Since *Tarasoff*

A survey study published in the *Stanford Law Review* indicates that psychiatrists and psychologists who responded to a questionnaire were aware of the *Tarasoff* decision. The study concluded that a potential victim was more likely to be warned by therapists after *Tarasoff* than prior to the decision. It was also noted that there was an increased likelihood of consultation with other professionals, and that recordkeeping had been changed. Some therapists stopped keeping detailed records, whereas others began keeping more detailed records to justify decisions that had been implemented.[35]

Many therapists have been appalled at the implications of the *Tarasoff* decision and feel it greatly impinges on the therapist-patient relationship. Wexler suggests that there might be some interesting therapeutic interventions as a result of this case. If the potential victim is a family member, that individual might be brought into the therapeutic situation, and a shift from an intrapsychic to an interactions model might be made. "Perhaps more precisely," Wexler notes, "Tarasoff may lead mental health professionals to practice the paradigm currently resisted but already accepted and preached by the bulk of the scientific and clinical literature."[36]

Beck interviewed 38 psychiatrists in the Boston area and asked them if they were aware of the *Tarasoff* decision and if they had warned a possible victim. In addition, they were asked whether they had discussed the warning with the patient prior to its issuance. Fourteen cases were found that justified warning. The impact of the warning on the therapeutic relationship was positive in two instances, and no apparent impact was noted in 12 cases. In four cases in which the warning was warranted and was not discussed ahead of time with the patient, the impact was negative. Beck concludes that "contrary to fears of *amici* and others, the warnings given seldom had an adverse effect on the therapeutic relationship."[37]

Beck emphasizes that when a patient communicates intended violence to a third party, "there is a distinction between a duty to assess violence according to a standard of reasonable care, which [therapists] could meet, and a duty to predict violence accurately which they cannot."[38] He concludes that therapists who can assess violence according to published standards would have a minute chance of being found liable for malpractice.

Mills et al. point out that the therapist should focus on imminent rather than future violence.[39] They suggest use of the Brief Psychiatric Rating Scale, which has been shown to be an indicator of violence subsequent to admission. Civil commitment should be initiated when the individual has indicated an inclination to violence. Records of prior hospitalizations should be carefully reviewed, and information from law enforcement officers should be recorded or communicated to persons authorizing discharge. Reasons for clinical interventions should be clearly documented. Finally, when third parties are threatened and the therapist is unsure whether the clinical interventions will prevent violence, the parties should be warned along with the local law enforcement agency.[40]

Because some cases have expanded the concept of a duty to unknown persons, some states have passed legislation limiting the responsibility of therapists. In California the following statute is in force:

> Psychotherapists; duty to warn of threatened violent behavior of patient; immunity from monetary liability
>
> (a) There shall be no monetary liability on the part of, and no cause of action shall rise against, any person who is a psychotherapist as defined in Section 1010 of the Evidence Code in failing to warn of and protect from a patient's threatened violent behavior or failing to predict and warn of and protect from a patient's violent behavior except where the patient has communicated to the psychotherapist a serious threat of physical violence against a reasonably identifiable victim or victims.
>
> (b) If there is a duty to warn and protect under the limited circumstances specified above, the duty shall be discharged by the psychotherapist making reasonable efforts to communicate the threat to the victim or victims and to a law enforcement agency.[41]

Nursing Implications. It is important to maintain confidential relationships with patients and clients. Nurses should establish whether or not the statutory privilege has been enacted by the legislature in their state and whether or not it includes nursing privilege. If a nurse does not have privileged communication, she should be especially alert for situations in which she might be compelled to testify or become subject to contempt of court if she refuses to testify.

Nurses working in the community should have consultants available if they assess someone in the home whom they think might become violent. In a community mental health center setting, there should be an established procedure concerning consultation and possible commitment proceedings for persons who are imminently, foreseeably dangerous. Since nurses frequently conduct group sessions for the chronically mentally ill, any change in behavior indicating potential violence should be brought to the attention of a physician for possible increase in medication, undertaking of commitment procedures, or the warning of third parties and possibly law enforcement agencies.

Nurses working in hospital settings should communicate any threats expressed by patients to other members of the therapeutic team. All information concerning violence in the community or at other hospitals should be in the record. Records from all treating facilities should be present. Although a significant number of patients have voluminous records, someone should be responsible for making sure that prior violence or admonitions from law enforcement personnel have been considered before discharge of the patient.

Those nurses working in private practice should have a consultant available to prescribe medications or help in initiating commitment. Careful documentation of issues or questions about potential violence should be recorded, and the clinical intervention employed should be carefully spelled out.

From decisions in the 1980s such as *Peck*, it is clear that not only psychiatrists but mental health professionals in general could be held to the standard to warn potential victims. Nursing as well as other disciplines should be cognizant of the legal implications of working with dangerous patients or clients.

Informed Consent

The right of an individual to be adequately informed about a procedure or treatment to be implemented by a health professional has long been established. However, only in the twentieth century has failure to obtain an informed consent resulted in increased litigation.[42] The consumer movement, along with the growing trend toward mental health clients questioning prescribed treatments, will focus even more attention on the issue of informed consent.

It is a basic premise that competent adults have the right to decide what they will authorize to be done to their own bodies.[43] Case law and published literature set out the following important components of informed consent: (1) An individual must be mentally competent and understand the procedures to which he is consenting.[44] (2) The individual must have enough information on which to base a decision, including any material risks. A risk is considered material when a reasonable person would "attach significance to the risk or cluster of risks in deciding whether or not to forego the proposed therapy."[45] Appelbaum remarks that in order to ascertain what a person would consider material to making a judgment about a procedure, "physicians are compelled to engage in a discussion with each patient." Appelbaum continues that the "fundamental goal of the idea of informed consent [is to] involve patients in decision making about their own care."[46] (3) There should also be a description of the available alternatives to the proposed treatment and the "dangers inherently and potentially involved in each."[47] The decision in *Natanson v. Kline* required not only disclosure of the treatment but the probability of success of that particular regimen.[48] (4) Consent can be withdrawn at any time.[49] (5) According to VanBiervliet and Sheldon-Wildgen, the more intrusive the procedure, the greater the need for informed consent.[50]

There are two exceptions to the requirement of informed consent and subsequent disclosure. The first exception applies to an unconscious patient whose condition would worsen without a particular procedure, when the benefit outweighs the potential harm of the proposed treatment plan.[51] The second exception applies when an individual would suffer severe detriment to his well-being as a result of disclosure.[52] In such a case, the physician may opt not to disclose the information in order to protect the patient. In view of the recent mental health consumer movement, this second exception should be carefully assessed.

One of the major problems in obtaining informed consent from mental health clients is their ability to comprehend the information that is given to them. Unless an individual has been found incompetent to manage his affairs or to make his own personal decisions, he is considered able to make decisions for himself. It is difficult, however, to maintain that a psychotic patient admitted voluntarily always has the understanding necessary to consent to treatment procedures. Ashley et al. point out that several authors have drawn attention to a "lack of comprehension on the part of a sample of mental patients as to the terms of their voluntary status."[53] However, this lack of comprehension was not limited to mental patients but was also observed in medical patients who knew less than the mental patients about their medication.[54] In a study conducted at a state mental hospital in Massachusetts, only 8.4% of 261 patients in a study group could give the name of at least one of their prescribed medications, including its frequency of administration and desired effect.[55] The Olins found that only 8% of residents at a state hospital could articulate the terms of their voluntary admission.[56]

Jaffe studied 16 psychiatric clinic outpatients and 16 outpatient medical patients through structured interviews. The degree of comprehension about short-term side effects of their medications was similar in the two groups, but the knowledge of both groups about long-term side effects was insufficient.[57] It is clear from these studies that health professionals will have to be diligent in providing information to clients so that the clients will be knowledgeable enough to give consent. After consent is obtained, health care personnel should be attuned to reinforcing information. Annas and Katz point out that there is some authority for a spouse to authorize consent for an incompetent patient.[58] In one case, the court ruled that a father could consent to treatment of an adult son with electroconvulsive therapy

(ECT).[59] In the case *In re Schuoler*, the Supreme Court of Washington ruled that the court must take into consideration a nonconsenting individual's wishes before making a substituted judgment to administer ECT. Additionally, the person's lawyer must be given adequate time to prepare for an ECT hearing.[60]

Annas and Katz conclude that in light of the recent movement for the rights of mental patients, it is prudent to have a legal guardian appointed, especially if the procedure is elective. They also suggest that it is the custom in the medical community to request consent of the next of kin. Although such consent may not be binding, it may waive the rights of the relative "to any future legal action."[61] In obtaining consent from an incompetent patient, legal advice should be sought if there is any question about whether the consent is valid.

Solomon suggests that in situations that involve involuntary patients, detailed written agreements or oral tape-recorded agreements should be made part of the permanent records. These would serve as contracts between patients and therapists and would be reviewed and renegotiated if necessary. In addition, it is suggested that these agreements be reviewed by an independent third party. Solomon points out that the feasibility of this kind of arrangement depends on the patient's condition, level of literacy, and willingness to participate.[62]

Traditionally, doctors have obtained informed consent for the procedures that they were to perform. Sometimes this responsibility is delegated to the nurse. If the nurse determines that the patient does not adequately understand the procedure the physician is to perform, the nurse should notify the physician or the appropriate administrator.[63] Mancini and Gale emphasize that if the procedure is to be performed by the nurse, consent should be obtained by the nurse.[64]

Zerubavel points out a very interesting phenomenon that may occur during the admission of a patient to a psychiatric facility. Since many mental health facilities utilize a team approach, each person on the team may assume that another team member has discussed with the patient the information relating to informed consent and the patient's rights. Zerubavel terms this "floating responsibility." He comments that physicians are personally responsible for patients, whereas nurses, because of shift changes, are not. "Nurses' responsibility for patients is almost entirely impersonal and is hardly ever expected to even transcend the temporal boundaries of their shifts."[65] Some would criticize this observation, but with the movement in many areas toward primary nursing, in which a single nurse is assigned responsibility for coordinating care of a patient during that patient's stay, the force of this criticism could be diminished.

Nursing Implications. Nurses should become acutely aware of the importance of providing information to clients about nursing procedures. If a client has questions pertaining to the procedure or to administration of medications, answers should be given as clearly and succinctly as possible. The client should be involved in the decision-making about procedures and the taking of medication. The nurse must be willing to clarify information and discuss questions on an ongoing basis. If queries arise concerning a medical procedure, the physician should be notified. It should also be noted that the client can revoke consent for a treatment or procedure at any time. The issue of medication and the right to refuse treatment is discussed later.

Guardianship and the Competency of the Individual

In most instances, individuals who have reached the age of 18 are permitted to manage their own property and health in any manner that they desire. Although a person may be functionally unable to make appropriate decisions regarding his health or finances, that person is still considered legally competent until a court declares him incompetent and appoints a guardian or conservator to act on his behalf as either guardian of his person, guardian of his estate, or both. All states have statutory provisions specifying the procedure and standards for declaring a person incompetent. Traditionally, the procedures have been informal and applied primarily to elderly or mentally disabled persons. There are also specific procedures for establishing guardianship of minors.

There is a confusing overlap between the use of commitment procedures to involuntarily hospitalize a mentally ill person for treatment and the process of declaring someone incompetent. Judicial and legislative actions limiting the role of psychiatric hospitals have resulted in a renewed focus on the utilization of guardianship procedures and the definition of incompetency. The basis for determining incompetency is a different issue from that of involuntary commitment to an inpatient psychiatric facility. However, in the past, persons who were involuntarily committed for treatment were often automatically declared incompetent as well.

By the 1960s most state statutes clearly separated the issues of competency and commitability; an individual who was involuntarily committed to a facility retained all his rights, including the right to manage his financial affairs. The only rights a person loses when involuntarily committed are the right to leave the facility and, until recently, the right to refuse psychiatric treatment. Some courts have now held that, under certain circumstances, an involuntarily committed person must be declared incompetent and a guardian appointed before treatment can be given against the person's will.

Ironically, the legal assault on the use of civil commitment and the emerging right of patients to refuse treatment have resulted in greater use of guardianship procedures. Many states have revised their guardianship and conservatorship laws to provide more stringent due process protection and a more specific definition of incompetency. The result of this reform has been the creation of a limited guardianship by which the court declares a person incompetent only in those areas in which he cannot function, rather than declaring him totally competent or incompetent. By 1980, 16 states had given judges the authority to limit the powers of the guardian, 10 had adopted limited guardianship statutes, and 8 more were considering such proposals.[66]

Although there is general agreement about the need for due process and stringent standards in guardianship proceedings, there is extensive disagreement about the role that guardians should play in seeking mental health care for their wards, particularly since the use of involuntary commitment has been greatly restricted. For example, a psychiatrist, Lee Haller, has stated that the appointment of a guardian is the solution to providing care to seriously mentally ill persons who refuse voluntary psychiatric treatment and who do not meet the involuntary commitment standards.[67] Haller suggests that a guardian will usually have the legal authority to "volunteer" the ward for treatment.

In fact, state laws vary regarding whether a guardian is specifically permitted or denied the power to commit his ward to a psychiatric facility if judicial commitment proceedings have not been initiated. Since the U.S. Supreme Court has not reviewed this issue, guardians in states where the statutes do not specify this exclusion are generally permitted to "voluntarily" admit their wards for psychiatric treatment. Some professionals, particularly lawyers, maintain that this procedure is an improper use of guardianship statutes because it is used to circumvent judicial commitment statutes.[68]

Schmidt and Peters surveyed the alleged need for guardians in the state of Florida. Mental hospitals, community mental health centers and clinics, developmental residential and institutional facilities, private and public receiving facilities, and aging and adult district offices reported that 11,147 persons needed legal guardians. They elucidate several points: State social service departments should seek to restore legal competency to those inappropriately declared incompetent; incompetent individuals without guardians should have adequate monitoring of their finances, and should have access to treatment programs.[69]

It has also been pointed out that the wording of some limited guardianship statutes has in fact expanded the use of limited guardianship to include individuals who previously would not have been declared incompetent.[70] Some lawyers have asserted that the use of guardianship is so arbitrary and so much abused that alternatives should be found.[71] However, it is unlikely that the use of guardianship will diminish unless the U.S. Supreme Court rules on the issue. Until then, it is important for health professionals to check the law of the state in which they are practicing.

Nursing Implications. The important point to remember is that a client is competent unless a court has declared him incompetent. Before beginning the treatment of any client, it is good practice to clarify whether or not a guardian has been appointed. If so, a copy of the court order should be obtained so that the limits of the guardian's authority will be clear. On the other hand, if a clearly incompetent client has not been declared legally incompetent, this information should be communicated to the administration of the facility and the family, and a determination should be made as to whether or not treatment can be provided.[72]

Power of Attorney

The power of attorney is a device that is occasionally suggested as a method of handling the affairs of and making decisions for a person who is mentally ill. A power of attorney is a written instrument authorizing one individual to act in the place of the person executing the document, in either a specific or an unlimited manner. This instrument has been used chiefly to facilitate the conducting of business when the primary person cannot be physically present. It is also frequently used for persons with physical limitations and elderly persons who wish to choose someone to handle their affairs and to avoid the necessity of conservatorship proceedings if they become ill.

In states that recognize a durable power of attorney, the device can be very useful in instances where an individual anticipates the possibility that he may become incompetent in the future, wishes to designate someone to handle his affairs, and wants to avoid the necessity of a family member seeking this authority from the court.[73] If a power of attorney specifically states that it will remain in effect if the person authorizing it becomes mentally disabled or otherwise incompetent, states authorizing a durable power of attorney will permit it to remain in effect. Additionally, such power of attorney may be drafted as a "springing" power of attorney, taking effect at some date in the future when the person executing it is determined by his attending physician to be incompetent.

The increased use of the power of attorney has raised the issue of whether it can also be used to designate a person to make health decisions for another person. Most jurisdictions— for example, New York—do not have explicit statutory authorization for delegation of the power to make health care decisions.[74] However, many doctors frequently accept such delegation in routine durable powers of attorney even without explicit statutory authorization. In New York, an attorney general's opinion has been issued that indicates that use of the power of attorney for this purpose in New York is not legal. A very few states have, in fact, legislated such authority.[75]

The power of attorney, of course, cannot be used for an individual who is already incompetent, since such a person is not competent to sign the document. This instrument should not be used to circumvent the guardianship statutes in these cases. Additionally, even if a state recognizes the use of this instrument for health care decisions, it is still highly unlikely that it can be used to authorize psychiatric treatment, particularly against the person's wishes.

Nursing Implications. It is important to remember that the power of attorney generally authorizes only the management of financial matters. Therefore, nurses presented with an instrument that attempts to authorize medical treatment should carefully review the statutory provisions in that state with the facility attorney or administrator.

Distinction Between Outpatient and Inpatient Care

The major distinction between outpatient and inpatient mental health care is that of voluntariness. In most states, outpatient mental health care is still provided on a voluntary basis only, as with any other form of health care. However, inpatient mental health care can be provided on either a voluntary or an involuntary basis. Therefore, when providing outpatient mental health care, the issues of informed consent and determining whether a person has been declared incompetent are very important. Some states have passed legislation permitting mandatory outpatient treatment under limited circumstances. The appropriate state law should be reviewed to assess whether such legislation exists.

The determination of "dangerousness" is an additional issue that has gained significance since the revised standards and procedures for involuntary commitment statutes have changed the ranges of behavior of clients currently served at the community level. Since fewer persons are hospitalized, and those who are hospitalized are detained for shorter periods, more potentially dangerous and chronic clients must be served on an outpatient basis. If a person appears to require inpatient care, the appropriate treatment should be discussed with the client so that he can make an informed decision, if possible. However, if the individual is unwilling to seek inpatient care or is posing an immediate threat of harm to himself or others, a decision must be reached concerning involuntary commitment to a psychiatric facility. Also, if a person poses a threat to a third party, a decision must be made whether or not to warn this party, as discussed previously in this chapter.

References

1. Ralph Slovenko: Accountability and Abuse of Confidentiality in the Practice of Psychiatry. *International Journal of Law and Psychiatry*, 2, no. 4, 1979, pp. 431–454.
2. Ibid., p. 447, ftn. 53.
3. Betty Holcomb: Varied State Laws Complicate Patient Record Privacy Issue. *Health Care Week*, January 1, 1979, p. 8. When You Apply for Insurance Is Your Life an Open Book? *U.S. News and World Report*, May 31, 1976, p. 33. William Hines: Medical Data Ethic Problems Eyed. *Chicago Sun-Times*, December 12, 1978, p. 24.
4. Samual Knapp and Leon VandeCreek: *Privileged Communications in the Mental Health Professions*. New York, Van Nostrand Reinhold, 1987, pp. 164–169.
5. *State v. Sweet*, 453 A.2d 1131 (Vt. 1982).
6. Ibid., at 1132.
7. *Myers v. State*, 310 S.E.2d 504 (Ga. 1984).
8. Knapp and VandeCreek: *Privileged Communications*, p. 75. *State v. Andring*, 342 N.W.2d 128 (Minn. 1984).
9. Knapp and VandeCreek: *Privileged Communications*, pp. 58–60.
10. Slovenko: *Accountability and Abuse*, p. 443.
11. American Medical Record Association: *Confidentiality of Patient Health Information*. Chicago, American Medical Record Association, 1977.
12. Seymour Halleck: *Law in the Practice of Psychiatry: A Handbook for Clinicians*. New York, Plenum Publishing Corp., 1980, p. 181.

13. Mary Cazalas: *Nursing and the Law*, 3rd ed. Germantown, Md., Aspen Systems Corp., 1978, p. 54.
14. Alan Westin: Medical Records: Should Patients Have Access? *The Hastings Center Report*, December 1977, pp. 23–28.
15. Halleck: *Law in the Practice of Psychiatry*, p. 181.
16. Eugene Stein, R.L. Furedy, M.J. Simonton and C.H. Neuffer: Patient Access to Medical Records on a Psychiatric Inpatient Unit. *American Journal of Psychiatry*, 136, no. 3, March 1979, pp. 327–329.
17. *Tarasoff v. Regents of the University of California*, 529 P.2d 553 (Cal. 1974) and 551 P.2d 334 (Cal. 1976).
18. *People v. Poddar*, 518 P.2d 342 (Cal. 1974).
19. Ibid., at 345.
20. Mark Mills, Greer Sullivan and Spencer Eth: Protecting Third Parties: A Decade After Tarasoff. *American Journal of Psychiatry*, 144, no. 1, January 1987, pp. 68–74.
21. *Tarasoff v. Regents of the University of California*, 551 P.2d 334 (Cal. 1976), at 347.
22. James Beck: The Psychotherapist's Duty to Protect Third Parties from Harm. *Mental and Physical Disability Law Reporter*, 11, no. 2, March-April 1987, pp. 141–148.
23. *McIntosh v. Milano*, 403 A.2d 500 (N.J. 1979).
24. Ebrahim J. Kermani and Sanford Drob: Tarasoff Decision: A Decade Later Dilemma Still Faces Psychotherapists. *American Journal of Psychotherapy*, 41, no. 2, April 1987, pp. 271–285, at 279.
25. *Peck v. The Counseling Service of Addison County, Inc.*, 449 A.2d 422 (Vt. 1985), at 422. See also *Currie v. United States*, 836 F.2d 209 (4th Cir. 1987); *Jablonski v. United States*, 712 F.2d 391 (9th Cir. 1983); *Bradley Center, Inc. v. Wessner*, 296 S.E.2d 693 (Ga. Ct. App. 1982); *Durflinger v. Artiles*, 564 F.Supp. 322 (D. Kan. 1981); *White v. United States*, 780 F.2d 97 (D.C. Cir. 1986); *Estate of Gilmore v. Buckley*, 787 F.2d 714 (1st Cir. 1986); *Davis v. Lhim*, 335 N.W. 2d 481 (Mich. App. 1983).
26. Alan A. Stone: Vermont Adopts Tarasoff: A Real Barn Burner. *American Journal of Psychiatry*, 143, no. 3, March 1986, pp. 352–355.
27. Arthur Bernstein: Some Legal Consequences of Treating Mental Patients. *Hospitals*, February 1981, p. 40.
28. *Thompson v. County of Alameda*, 614 P.2d 728 (Cal. 1980).

29. *Shaw v. Glickman*, 415 A.2d 625 (Md. Ct. Spec. App. 1980). See also *Hedlund v. Orange County*, 669 P.2d 41 (Cal. Sup. Ct. 1983).
30. *Lipari v. Sears Roebuck & Co.*, 497 F.Supp. 185 (D. Neb. 1980) at 193.
31. Beck: The Psychotherapist's Duty, p. 145.
32. Ibid.
33. *Petersen v. State*, 671 P.2d 230 Wash. 1983).
34. Beck: The Psychotherapist's Duty, p. 145.
35. Note, *Stanford Law Review*, 31, November 1978, p. 165.
36. David Wexler: Patients, Therapists and Third Parties: The Victimological Virtues of Tarasoff. *International Journal of Law and Psychiatry*, 2, 1974, pp. 1–28, at 28.
37. James C. Beck: When the Patient Threatens Violence: An Empirical Study of Clinical Practice After Tarasoff. *Bulletin of the American Academy of Psychiatry and Law*, 10, no. 3, 1983, pp. 189–201.
38. Beck: The Psychotherapist's Duty, p. 147.
39. Mills, Sullivan and Eth: Protecting Third Parties, p. 74.
40. Ibid.
41. California Civil Code §43.92.
42. Paul Appelbaum, Charles Lidz and Alan Meisel: *Informed Consent: Legal Theory and Clinical Practice*, New York, Oxford University Press, 1987, p. 37.
43. *Schloendorff v. Society of New York Hospital*, 105 N.E. 92 (N.Y. 1914).
44. Marguerite Mancini and Alice T. Gale: *Emergency Care and the Law*, Rockville, Md., Aspen Systems Corp., 1981, p. 88.
45. *Canterbury v. Spence*, 464 F.2d 772 (D.C. Cir. 1972), at 787.
46. Appelbaum, Lidz and Meisel: *Informed Consent*, p. 46.
47. *Cobbs v. Grant*, 502 P.2d 1 (Cal. 1972), at 10.
48. *Natanson v. Kline*, 350 P.2d 1093 (Kan. 1960).
49. Mancini and Gale: *Emergency Care*, p. 88.
50. Alan VanBiervliet and Jan Sheldon-Wildgen: *Liability Issues in Community Based Programs*, Baltimore, Paul H. Brookes Publishing Co., 1981, p. 124.
51. *Canterbury v. Spence*, at 788.
52. Ibid., at 789.

53. Mary Ashley, Regina Sestak and Loren Roth: Legislating Human Rights: Informed Consent and the Pennsylvania Mental Health Procedures Act. *Bulletin of the American Academy of Psychiatry and the Law*, 8, no. 2, 1981, pp. 133–151, at 134.

54. Ibid.

55. Jeffrey Geller: State Hospital Patients and Their Medication–Do They Know What They Take? *American Journal of Psychiatry*, 139, no. 5, May 1982, pp. 611–615.

56. Grace Olin and Harry S. Olin: Informed Consent in Voluntary Mental Hospital Admissions. *American Journal of Psychiatry*, 132, no. 9, September 1975, pp. 938–941.

57. Robert Jaffe: Problems of Long-Term Informed Consent. *Bulletin of the American Academy of Psychiatry and Law*, 14, no. 2, 1986, pp. 163–169. See also Diane Kjervik: The Psychiatric Nurse's Duty to Warn Potential Victims of Homicidal Psychotherapy Outpatients. *Law, Medicine and Health Care*, 9, no. 6, December 1981, pp. 11–16.

58. George J. Annas and Barbara F. Glantz Katz: *The Rights of Doctors, Nurses and Allied Health Professionals*, Cambridge, Mass., Ballinger Publishing Co., 1981, p. 79.

59. *Farver v. Olkon*, 254 P.2d 520 (Cal. 1953).

60. *In re Schuoler* 723 P.2d 1103 (Wash. 1986).

61. Annas and Katz: *The Rights of Doctors*, p. 80.

62. Trudy Solomon: Informed Consent for Mental Patients. *Human Rights*, 31, Spring 1979, pp. 31–32, 52–55.

63. Angela Holder and John Lewis: Informed Consent and the Nurse. *Nursing Law and Ethics*, 2, no. 2, 1981, pp. 1, 2, 8.

64. Mancini and Gale: *Emergency Care*, p. 88.

65. Eviatar Zerubavel: The Bureaucratization of Responsibility: The Case of Informed Consent. *Bulletin of the American Academy of Psychiatry and the Law*, 8, no. 2, 1981, pp. 161–167.

66. Report of Committee on Legal Incapacity. Limited Guardianship: Survey of Implementation Considerations. *Real Property, Probate and Trust Journal*, 15, 1980, pp. 544–556. See also Support Services and Alternatives to Guardianship. *Mental and Physical Disability Law Reporter*, 12, no. 4, March-April 1988, pp. 207–228.

67. Lee H. Haller: Guardianship: An Alternative to I'm Sorry. *Bulletin of the American Academy of Psychiatry and the Law*, 7, no. 3, 1979, pp. 296–305.

68. G.H. Morris: The Use of Guardianships to Achieve—or to Avoid—the Least Restrictive Alternative. *International Journal of Law and Psychiatry*, 3, 1980, pp. 97–115, at 99.
69. Winsor C. Schmidt and Roger Peters: Legal Incompetents' Need for Guardians in Florida. *Bulletin of the American Academy of Psychiatry and the Law*, 15, no. 1, 1986, pp. 69–83.
70. Morris: The Use of Guardianships, p. 107.
71. G. Alexander: Premature Probate: A Different Perspective on Guardianship for the Elderly. *Stanford Law Review*, 31, 1979, pp. 1003–1033.
72. See the following article on Individual Functional Assessment developed for extended care facilities: Arpiar G. Saunders, Jr., and Mitchell M. Simon: Individual Functional Assessment: An Instruction Manual. *Mental and Physical Disability Law Reporter*, 11, no. 1, 1987, pp. 60–70.
73. Tennessee Code Annotated 34-6-102.
74. Dale A. Moore: The Durable Power of Attorney as Alternative to the Improper Use of Conservatorship for Health Care Decision Making, *St. John Law Review*, 60, Summer 1986, p. 654.
75. *California Civil Code* 2430-2444 (Deering 1986); *Delaware Code Annotated* Title 16, Sections 2501(b), (c) 1983; *Pennsylvania Const. Statutes Annotated* Section 20-5603(h) (Purdon Supp. 1986).

CHAPTER 3

Admissions to Psychiatric Facilities

Least Restrictive Alternative

One of the issues confronting a mental health professional treating a mentally ill person is whether to refer the individual to an inpatient facility. Broadly, mental health inpatient admissions can be classified into three categories: voluntary, emergency involuntary, and indefinite involuntary (judicial or civil commitment).

Each type of admission has legal implications about which mental health professionals should be aware. However, prior to any commitment, the doctrine of the "least restrictive alternative" must be addressed. The concept of the least restrictive alternative means providing sufficient care for the client with the least restrictive methods in the least restrictive setting. The application of this idea to an inpatient setting is discussed in Chapter 4.

One of the first mental health cases to invoke the concept of the least restrictive alternative was *Lake v. Cameron*.[1] An elderly woman filed a writ of habeas corpus requesting her release from an institution in Washington, D.C. Although her mental health caregivers felt that she needed attention and not constant medical supervision, she was nevertheless continuously hospitalized. The court held that alternatives to confinement in a mental hospital should be investigated, including "outpatient, foster care, half-way houses, day hospitals and nursing homes."[2]

In a later class action suit in the District of Columbia, the court ruled that "suitable care and treatment under the least restrictive conditions are required."[3] In this case, the government was mandated to develop less restrictive alternatives if such alternatives were not already available. In *O'Connor v. Donaldson*, the U.S. Supreme Court commented that one cannot constitutionally be confined if other less restrictive alternatives are more suitable and if the person has a support system and is capable of safely surviving in the community.[4] Few statutes define which persons shall be responsible for developing and assessing therapeutic treatment alternatives.[5] Most state commitment laws now authorize commitment only if there are no less restrictive alternatives available. However, when developing a treatment plan for an individual, *all* alternatives should be outlined, including inpatient and community treatment options. This would include analysis of the full range of alternatives, from the least to the most restrictive.

If commitment is necessary, the professionals who provide evidence at a commitment hearing should be able to list treatment alternatives in the region. Treatment options will vary depending on the location of the individual. For example, a halfway house or a day care center may not exist in a rural county, but they might be available in a neighboring area.

Types of Admissions

There are three basic types of admissions to inpatient psychiatric facilities: (1) voluntary admission, (2) emergency commitment, and (3) indefinite commitment (civil commitment).[6] State laws pertaining to admissions procedures apply to both public and private facilities. Of course, voluntary admission is more familiar to most nurses because this is the only method of admission to general medical facilities. However, because of the nature of the illness of some psychiatric patients, the procedures related to voluntary admission must be handled with particular care.

Voluntary Admission

State laws may vary as to the procedures allowed to be used for voluntary admission, but they all provide for the admission of persons who voluntarily request services. Usually the statute states that any person can be admitted to a psychiatric facility as a voluntary patient if he is mentally ill, in need of inpatient care, and willing to seek admission.[7] However, as a result of the increased emphasis on community treatment and the provision of services through the least restrictive alternative, a person seeking inpatient care may be referred to a community mental health center for care unless his condition or behavior requires immediate hospitalization. Additionally, the number of beds in state mental hospitals has been significantly reduced; consequently, potential inpatients will be carefully screened by admitting professionals. Most private institutions will accept voluntary admission upon the referral of the treating physician.

Just as all patients must consent to admission to a general medical facility and to any subsequent treatment, the psychiatric patient must also provide such consent. However, some commentators have questioned whether all psychiatric patients have the capacity to understand and to consent to such admission and treatment.[8] One state has resolved this dilemma by recognizing the informal admission, which has the same legal status as a medical admission.[9] An informal admission indicates that the patient is agreeable to admission and that no one will detain him if he insists upon leaving; however, most nurses practice in states where only the option of a voluntary admission is available.

The consent to voluntary admission and treatment consists of three elements: (1) sufficient information to enable the individual to make an informed decision, (2) the absence of coercion to ensure the voluntariness of the decision, and (3) the patient's competency to make the decision.[10] The first two elements can be addressed by designing procedures and forms to demonstrate that the person was provided with sufficient information and that he was not coerced. The problems associated with these two elements do not vary greatly between medical patients and psychiatric patients.[11] Competency, the third element of informed consent, is of particular relevance to the admission of psychiatric patients because mental illness is the most likely of all illnesses to affect competency.[12] Because voluntary entry to a psychiatric facility is the first point at which most seriously ill patients are asked to give informed consent, this procedure must be handled with care.

If a person is thought to be incompetent to consent to his own admission to a psychiatric facility, the only immediately available option is emergency commitment. However, since the condition and behavior of many mentally ill persons do not meet emergency commitment standards, this option has limited use. Another alternative is to initiate guardianship proceedings so that a guardian can consent to the admission. However, as discussed in Chapter 2, some state statutes prohibit the guardian from consenting to admission of the ward to a psychiatric facility and require that commitment proceedings be used for this purpose. Even if the guardian can legally consent to the admission, seeking guardianship is a timely and costly procedure that will not provide an immediate solution for a person who needs hospitalization.

In practice, most psychiatric facilities maintain that a person must be presumed competent if he has not been legally adjudicated incompetent by a court of law. Therefore, emphasis is placed on the procedure of informing the patient of the terms of his admission and the care he will be receiving, as well as on the procedure for documenting that the patient was not coerced. However, if there is serious question about a person's competency to consent to admission, and if the person meets commitment standards, the involuntary commitment process should be initiated. Otherwise most state statutes provide no viable options.

Once a person has been voluntarily admitted to a psychiatric facility, he must continue to provide consent for treatment. Unlike committed patients, there is no question of whether or not a voluntary patient has the right to refuse treatment. If a voluntary patient refuses treatment, the facility must find another method of treatment agreeable to the patient, release the patient, or, if the patient poses a danger to himself or others, initiate commitment proceedings.

All state statutes provide for a voluntary patient to be released within a specified period if he requests release. For example, Tennessee state law requires that such a patient be released within 12 hours of his request to leave.[13] If the staff considers the person to pose a danger to himself or others as a result of his mental illness, the director of the facility should initiate commitment proceedings.

Emergency Commitment

When an individual is unwilling to seek treatment and poses an immediate threat of serious harm to himself or others as a result of mental illness, state statutes provide for emergency involuntary admission to a psychiatric facility. This commitment differs from indefinite judicial commitment because it permits commitments for a short period without a court hearing. Because of the potential for abuse, the standards and procedures for emergency commitment have been reviewed in a number of court decisions.[14]

Most states require some showing of dangerousness. There has been a great deal of debate on whether mental health professionals can predict dangerousness. Miller reports that, in a review of the literature on dangerousness, especially of methodologically sound research studies, only 50% of clinical predictions of dangerousness for acute patients were found to be accurate, and this percentage decreased for individuals hospitalized for a long period of time.[15]

Rachlin reviewed a selection of reported appellate court decisions from seven states. He concludes that the definition of dangerousness is being extended. For example, a Texas court decided in one case that an individual could not make a logical decision to be treated and that not to intervene would cause severe suffering.[16] One woman was committed after she wrote letters that did not make sense; the court said that the state does not have to wait until the danger is imminent and acute to act.[17] Some states, however, require a more overt act of dangerousness before commitment.

The state of New York expanded its laws between 1978 and 1984 to include commitment predicated on mental illness and the need for treatment. A study conducted on the results of this change in legislation showed evidence of procedural protections being reduced, and the author of the study reports that the control given to clinicians without judicial oversight was too great.[18]

Usually, when a person is thought to require emergency hospitalization and refuses to seek treatment, a law enforcement official or a licensed physician is authorized by law to take the person into custody for the purpose of having him undergo a psychiatric evaluation and, if recommended by the examining physician, to provide transportation to a psychiatric facility. For example, under Tennessee law, a facility is authorized to admit a person as an emergency case if a physician or PhD clinical psychologist certifies that the person's behavior meets the standards for emergency commitment.[19] In addition, the admitting facility must provide a physician to certify that the person meets these standards. Once these two certifications have been provided, the facility may admit the person for up to five days before a probable cause hearing is held.

After the probable cause hearing, the judge must either order the patient released or order that the patient be held only for a specific period, for example, no more than 20 days after initial detention in Tennessee. At the end of that time, the person must be released unless a petition for indefinite commitment has been filed. It is important that the staff in the facility advise the person of the nature of his commitment and his rights under this commitment, as well as scrupulously follow the procedural requirements set out in the commitment statute.

Under most state laws, aversive therapy, such as electroconvulsive therapy, is not permitted during emergency commitment. Generally the only care permitted is the routine treatment necessitated by the emergency condition of the patient. If at any time during the commitment the person's condition improves so that he no longer meets the emergency standards, he should be released or permitted to admit himself voluntarily.

Indefinite Commitment (Civil Commitment)

The third type of admission procedure is the indefinite commitment, otherwise known as judicial or civil commitment. This is the only process by which a person may be detained in a psychiatric facility against his will for an indefinite period. Most state legislatures have responded to the legal attacks on this procedure by making extensive revisions in the state commitment statutes.

The legal and historical justification for the use of indefinite commitment has been based on two theories: the *parens patriae* power of the state to take care of persons who are unable to take care of themselves, and the policy power of the state to protect the public from dangerous individuals.[20] Originally, most commitment statutes relied on both theories and provided for the detention of individuals who were dangerous as well as of individuals who simply required care because of their mental illness and refused to seek treatment.[21] Some court cases in the 1970s focused on the question of whether a state could constitutionally commit a person who had not exhibited dangerous behavior.[22] In other words, they speculated that only the police power and not the *parens patriae* power of the state could be relied on to justify indefinite commitment. However, other courts have justified the *parens patriae* commitment on the basis that treatment would be provided.

In addition to the issues raised concerning the behavior required for commitment, the procedures used for the commitment process have also been scrutinized by the courts. Under most state statutes, this process can be initiated when an authorized official, physician, or family member files a petition for such commitment along with certification by two physicians (or mental health professionals, if provided by statute) that the individual is mentally ill, that his behavior poses a likelihood of serious harm, and that suitable community resources are unavailable. In spite of the argument that courts should limit commitments to dangerous persons, the standards for "likelihood of serious harm" generally are broader for indefinite commitment than for emergency commitment. The standards include immediate danger to self or others as well as more passive types of danger that can result from a person's inability to avoid or protect himself from harm because of mental illness. Some legal experts argue that because commitment results in the deprivation of liberty, the procedures used should parallel those used for criminal trials. Certain authorities have gone so far as to suggest that the commitment process be abolished.[23]

Obviously, these are issues that will ultimately have to be resolved by the U.S. Supreme Court. The first case to be decided by the court that involved a review of the conditions under which a mental patient may be involuntarily committed, other than in relation to criminal charges, was *O'Connor v. Donaldson* in 1974,[24] the specifics of which are fully discussed in Chapter 4. Although the court was asked to review the right to treatment in this case, the court sidestepped this issue. The court did, however, state the following about the requirements for confinement:

> Mere public intolerance or animosity cannot constitutionally justify the deprivation of a person's physical liberty. In short, a state cannot constitutionally confine without more a nondangerous individual who is capable of surviving safely in freedom by himself or with the help of willing and responsible family members or friends.[25]

By focusing attention on certain minimal requirements for confinement, the court delayed having to make a decision about the right to treatment. The court neither defined the "more" required to confine the nondangerous mentally ill nor stipulated whether anything more is required to confine dangerously mentally ill individuals or those not capable of surviving safely in freedom with help from family and friends.[26]

Not until five years later, in 1979, did the Supreme Court again decide another civil commitment case. In *Addington v. Texas*, the court reviewed a variety of procedural issues in indefinite commitment.[27] The major issue presented in that case was the standard of proof required by the Constitution. Chief Justice Burger, who authored the opinion, reached a compromise between applying the standard used in a criminal trial and the standard used in a civil trial. He reasoned that the risk of an erroneous decision in civil commitment proceedings requires the use of a standard of persuasion more rigorous than the "preponderance of the evidence" standard used in civil proceedings, but that the "beyond a reasonable doubt" standard required in criminal cases was unnecessary because the state sought to help, not punish. [28] He therefore settled on the "clear and convincing" standard, a burden of proof that requires more than a "preponderance of the evidence" but less than "beyond a reasonable doubt."

The court further held that the substantive standards for civil commitment for mental illness may vary from state to state, and that procedures must be allowed to vary as long as they meet the constitutional minimum. The opinion held that the state has a legitimate interest under its *parens patriae* powers to provide care for its citizens who are unable to care for themselves because of mental illness, and that the state also has authority under its police power to protect the community from the dangerous tendencies of those who are mentally ill. Because Burger relied on the theory that the purpose of commitment laws is to help the person rather than to punish him, *Addington* leaves unclear whether or not a person who is committed only because he is dangerous should be treated any differently from a person who is committed because of his need for care. Therefore, the case does not resolve the questions left unanswered by *O'Connor*.

A 1987 decision, *Streicker v. Prescott*, concerned residents of St. Elizabeth's Hospital in Washington, D.C. A federal court ruled that all patients confined prior to 1973 would have to be provided with a hearing because their commitments were predicated on the standard of preponderance of the evidence, a lesser standard than clear and convincing evidence, which is now the law.[29]

Justice Burger expanded on his position in a concurring opinion in *Youngberg v. Romeo*, a case concerning a person involuntarily committed to an institution for the mentally retarded. In this opinion, Burger specifically stated his belief that there is no constitutional right to "habilitation."[30] Because the concept of habilitation for a mentally retarded individual is parallel to the concept of treatment for a mentally ill person, this case is pertinent to this issue. The majority opinion held that the individual had a right to minimally adequate or reasonable training to ensure safety and freedom from undue restraint. However, the court once again declined to rule on whether or not an individual involuntarily committed to a state institution has some general constitutional right to training per se.

New Civil Commitment Guidelines

The National Center for State Courts, through its Institute on Mental Disability and the Law, has developed guidelines for involuntary civil commitment.[31] Wexler writes that several assumptions were adopted before generating the guidelines: Proposals for reform should come from a multidisciplinary group. Guidelines, rather than model legislation, are the best means for initiating changes in the civil commitment process. The concern of the task force was over procedural implementation of the law rather than what statutes were on the books. Reforms should be based on actual problems and on models already in existence. Those involved in the system, such as judges and lawyers, need to know how the mental health system works in practice.[32]

The guidelines are very comprehensive and should be reviewed by legislators and mental health personnel anticipating a change in commitment laws in their states. Some interesting recommendations include developing a community coordinating council made up of individuals from several disciplines plus patients, family, and volunteer groups who would address common problems in the system. It is suggested that communities develop a services directory listing agencies, self-help groups, and other service organizations in order to assist in providing continuity of care. The report notes that many states mandate a continuum of services for continuity of care, but that theory and practice are not one and the same. The report concludes, "The mental health-justice system has yet to develop services to match the spectrum of needs of persons presented to it."

Sections of the guidelines include procedures for creating a screening agency and developing a relationship with law enforcement officers. Guidelines for mental health examination, including procedures for implementation and developing reports, legal representation, the court hearings, judicial determinations, and case dispositions as well as posthearing procedures, are set forth in the report.[33]

Involuntary Outpatient Commitment

The terms *preventive commitment, involuntary outpatient commitment,* and *mandatory outpatient commitment* have been used to describe a process whereby an individual is required to attend and submit to therapeutic meetings and interventions in the community. Stefan describes outpatient commitment as providing for less restrictive alternatives in the community rather than treatment in an inpatient facility.[34] Preventive commitment requires that the following criteria be met: Without treatment the individual will exhibit symptomatology that will meet the requirements for commitment to an institution; there is a mental illness present, and the ramifications of that illness cause the person to refrain from seeking voluntary treatment.[35] Various states have different requirements. North Carolina law dictates that the individual must be able to live safely in the community with an adequate support system.[36] The doctrine of *parens patriae* enables the state to intervene in the best interests of individuals who are not able to adequately care for their mental illness.

One of the major rationales for instigating some kind of treatment control over the individual after hospitalization is that the nature of major mental illness causes the individual to be prone to exacerbations of the disorder upon discharge if a therapeutic regimen is not followed. There have been numerous objections to this concept, however. After a review of state statutes, Stefan concludes that "states fall short of granting outpatients the same procedural protections provided to inpatients."[37] Mulvey and associates write that threats of state action against a client "rarely provide effective therapy but quickly come to serve social monitoring functions instead."[38] Another issue is the inadequacy of treatment alternatives available in some states' community mental health clinics. Lack of resources to develop the kind of staffing patterns needed has been set forth as an explanation of the failure to offer a wide range of services. Mulvey et al. remark that many have questioned "whether the programs have thus actually failed or have just never really been tried."[39]

There is also the issue of quality control. A variety of disciplines practice in institutional settings, so that monitoring of care is easier to scrutinize, whereas outpatient care is more private and concealed.[40]

Advocates of involuntary outpatient commitment argue that it is better to treat individuals in the community, where a psychosocial approach can be implemented, rather than institutionalize them and face all of the problems associated with dependency. Mulvey et al. write that outpatient commitment provides an opportunity for persons with psychoses to have the experience of living in the community when their illness is in remission, which for some chronically mentally ill clients has only occurred in inpatient facilities.[41]

In reviewing some reports on the results of outpatient commitment, researchers in North Carolina write of the success of their programs. The criteria are specifically spelled out, and the extent of the commitment is initially limited to 90 days, with a possible extension to 180 days and a further continuation for one year if the court so determines. One of the major differences in criteria for inpatient as opposed to outpatient commitment is the elimination of the standard of dangerousness for community care. A $2,000 reimbursement for each client who is mandated to outpatient commitment is provided to the mental health center.[42] Scheid-Cook reports that those individuals ordered to outpatient commitment are usually chronically mentally ill, with a history of many hospitalizations.[43] Another report from the same state indicates that researchers believe that mandatory outpatient treatment is successful because it does keep clients coming for treatment, and medication compliance is high. It is noted, however, that some individuals placed on mandatory outpatient commitment never do come to the mental health center, and others are removed from the commitment by the staff of the center.[44]

One psychotherapist, in a detailed account of therapeutic work with a highly suicidal individual manifesting severe borderline symptomatology, details the experience of working with an angry patient who is committed to outpatient treatment. She concludes that the procedure can be useful in substituting for the client the security of outpatient commitment rather than long-term hospitalization.[45]

Mulvey et al. suggest that a middle-of-the-road stance can be taken on outpatient commitment. Noting that "liberty is a treasure to be guarded but not worshipped,"[46] and that sometimes some coercion is desirable to prevent human suffering, they recommend that guidelines for involuntary commitment be clearly delineated, and that the persons subjected to this form of treatment have a history of exacerbations of illness accompanied by high response to intervention. Mulvey et al. also recommend that a time interval be established, based on the patient's previous intervals between relapses, when state monitoring will occur. They also advise that incompetency as related to refusal of treatment should be adjudicated at the outpatient commitment hearing. They suggest that hearings be held in a courtroom setting rather than at a treatment facility to minimize the ease of recommending someone for this form of treatment.[47]

Tennessee passed a mandatory outpatient commitment statute in 1981. The authors believe that it has not met with success, as the community mental health centers, mental health institutes, and law enforcement agencies were not consulted prior to the enactment of the law. (Tennessee defines its law as a conditional release and not as preventive commitment.) Law enforcement officers are reluctant to pick up and detain individuals for reinstitutionalization; therefore, mental health center staff hesitate to implement the initial action to bring the individual to the hospital for treatment. Results of this law indicate that repeat hospitalizations have not diminished.[48]

Nursing Implications. Nurses in both outpatient and inpatient facilities must become acquainted with the various admission statutes in their state as well as admission procedures developed by the individual facilities where they practice. The type of admission for each patient should be clearly identified in the record, because the procedures for treatment and requests to leave the facility may be handled differently depending on the admission status of the patient. Before the patient's admission to the facility, procedures and statutory requirements should be carefully implemented and documented. If the institution is not following the law, the nurse should bring this fact to the attention of the administrators.

In some states nurses are recognized by commitment statutes as being qualified to certify the need for commitment; however, in the majority of states other professionals are designated for this assignment. Nurses working in the community may well be the caregivers. They identify outpatient clients needing hospitalization or dangerous voluntary patients requesting to leave the facility. Commitment standards may vary in their application, particularly if a client retains a knowledgeable, aggressive attorney. The outcome of commitment proceedings is not always predictable. However, nurses have the responsibility for recommending commitment proceedings for individuals whose condition, in their opinion, requires hospitalization. Therefore, it is imperative to describe behavior accurately and record it definitively in the patient's record. Mental health professionals may not always agree with the outcome of a commitment hearing; however, the patient has the right to have all information relative to his condition accurately assessed before he is involuntarily detained in an institution.

AIDS and the Psychiatric Setting

Appelbaum has raised the issue of possible commitment of AIDS patients to a psychiatric facility to prevent them from spreading their disease.[49] Quarantining of individuals has not been common in recent decades because most major communicable diseases have been brought under control through immunization and other forms of prevention. Would preventive commitment for AIDS be legitimate use of the commitment process? If the person does not present with a mental illness, the commitment could be easily questioned. The authors know of one instance in which an individual with AIDS was committed to a mental hospital to prevent sexual acting out and spread of the disease. The person later developed severe mental problems, and at this point the commitment was justified. It is not unusual for individuals suffering from AIDS to exhibit symptoms of suicide, depression, and dementia in the later stages of the disease.[50] Hospitalization of AIDS patients on psychiatric units is going to present a challenge for nursing in the 1990s. A group of authors write, "Members of all disciplines must cope with a significant cognitive and emotional strain: keeping up to date in a burgeoning field of knowledge; tolerating legal, ethical, and scientific ambiguity; and working with patients who are dying before their eyes."[51]

References

1. *Lake v. Cameron*, 364 F.2d 657 (D.C. Cir. 1966 en banc).
2. Ibid., at 659–660.

3. *Dixon v. Weinberger*, 406 F.Supp. 974 (D.C. Cir. 1975), at 979.
4. *O'Connor v. Donaldson*, 422 U.S. 563 (1975), at 575.
5. P. Browning Hoffman and Lawrence L. Foust: Least Restrictive Treatment of the Mentally Ill: A Doctrine in Search of Its Senses. *San Diego Law Review* 14, July 1977, pp. 110–1154, at 1119.
6. M.D. Hemelt and M.E. Mackert: *Dynamics of Law in Nursing and Health Care*, Reston, Va., Reston Publishing Co., 1978, pp. 101–102. See also Tennessee Code Annotated, 33-6-101, 33-6-102, and 33-6-103.
7. *Tennessee Code Annotated*, 33-6-101.
8. Harold Owens: When Is Voluntary Commitment Really Voluntary? *American Journal of Psychiatry*, 134, no. 1, January 1977, pp. 104–110.
9. Ibid., p. 109.
10. Paul S. Appelbaum, Stuart A. Mirkin, Alan L. Bateman: Empirical Assessment of Competency to Consent to Psychiatric Hospitalization. *American Journal of Psychiatry*, 138, no. 9, September 1981, pp. 1170–1176.
11. Ibid.
12. Ibid.
13. *Tennessee Code Annotated*, 33-6-101.
14. *Yezerski v. Fong*, 428 A.2d 766 (Pa. Comm. Ct. 1981). See also *Williams v. Meredith*, 407 A.2d 569 (D.C. Ct. App. 1979).
15. Robert D. Miller: *Involuntary Civil Commitment of the Mentally Ill in the Post-Reform Era*. Springfield, Ill., Charles C Thomas, 1987, p. 24.
16. Stephen Rachlin: Redefining Dangerousness for Civil Commitment. *Hospital and Community Psychiatry*, 38, no. 8, August 1987, pp. 884–887. *Johnson v. State*, 693 S.W.2d 559 (Tex. App. 4th Dist. 1985).
17. *Matter of Mazzara*, 478 N.E.2d 567 (Ill. App. 4th Dist. 1985).
18. Miller: Involuntary Civil Commitment, p. 43.
19. *Tennessee Code Annotated*, 33-6-603.
20. Richard B. Saphire: The Civilly-Committed Public Mental Patient and the Right to Aftercare. *Florida State University Law Review*, 4, 1976, pp. 232–295.
21. Ibid., p. 255.
22. T.S. Szasz: *Law, Liberty and Psychiatry*. New York, Macmillan Co., 1963.

23. *Lessard v. Schmidt*, 349 F.Supp. 1078 (E. D. Wis., 1974), vacated on procedural grounds 421 U.S. 957 (1975), reinstated 413 F.Supp. 1318 (E. D. Wis., 1976).
24. *O'Connor v. Donaldson*, 493 F.2d 507 (5th Cir., 1974), vacated on other grounds 422 U.S. 563 (1975).
25. *O'Connor v. Donaldson*, 422 U.S. 563 (1975), at 575–576.
26. Daniel Shurman: Warren Burger and the Civil Commitment Tetralogy. *International Journal of Law and Psychiatry*, 3, 1980, pp. 155–161 (see especially p. 156).
27. *Addington v. Texas*, 441 U.S. 418, 434 (1979), at 434.
28. Shurman: Warren Burger, p. 157.
29. *Mental and Physical Disability Law Reporter*, 11, no. 4, July-August 1987, pp. 224–225. *Streicker v. Prescott*, C.A. no. 84-1538 (D.D.C., May 19, 1987).
30. *Youngberg v. Romeo*, 102 Sup. Ct. 2452 (1982).
31. National Center for State Courts' Guidelines for Involuntary Civil Commitment. *Mental and Physical Disability Law Reporter*, 10, no. 5, September-October 1986, pp. 409–514.
32. David Wexler: Reforming the Law in Action Through Empirically Grounded Civil Commitment Guidelines. *Hospital and Community Psychiatry*, 39, no. 4, April 1988, pp. 402–405.
33. National Center for State Courts' Guidelines, pp. 409–514.
34. Susan Stefan: Preventive Commitment: The Concept and Its Pitfalls. *Mental and Physical Disability Law Reporter*, 11, no. 4, July-August 1987, pp. 288–302, at 288.
35. Ibid.
36. Ibid.
37. Ibid., p. 292.
38. Edward Mulvey, Jeffrey Geller and Loren Roth: The Promise and Peril of Involuntary Commitment. *American Psychologist*, 42, no. 6, June 1987, pp. 575–584, at 575.
39. Ibid.
40. Ibid., at p. 576.
41. Ibid., at p. 578.
42. Virginia Aldigé Hiday and Teresa L. Scheid-Cook: The North Carolina Experience with Outpatient Commitment: A Critical Appraisal. *International Journal of Law and Psychiatry*, 10, 1987, pp. 215–232.

43. Teresa L. Scheid-Cook: Commitment of the Mentally Ill to Outpatient Treatment. *Community Mental Health Journal*, 23, no. 3, Fall 1987, pp. 173–182, at 180.
44. Hiday and Scheid-Cook: The North Carolina Experience, pp. 229–230.
45. Kathleen Schneider-Braus: Civil Commitment to Outpatient Psychotherapy: A Case Study. *Bulletin of the American Academy of Psychiatry and the Law*, 14, no. 3, 1986, pp. 273–279.
46. Mulvey, Geller and Roth: The Promise and Peril, p. 579.
47. Ibid., pp. 579–582.
48. Stefan: Preventive Commitment, p. 291.
49. Paul S. Appelbaum: AIDS, Psychiatry, and the Law. *Hospital and Community Psychiatry*, 39, no. 1, January 1988, pp. 13–14.
50. J.W. Baer, J.M. Hall, K. Holm and S. Lewitter-Koehler: Challenges in Developing an Inpatient Psychiatric Program for Patients with AIDS and ARC. *Hospital and Community Psychiatry*, 38, no. 12, December 1987, pp. 1299–1303.
51. Ibid., p. 1303.

CHAPTER 4

The Rights of Patients in Institutions

When individuals are hospitalized in a mental health facility, they may be deprived of the freedom to leave the facility, but they do maintain certain legal rights. These rights are usually defined by state law, and nurses should determine what rights are specified by the law in the state in which they practice. Of course, unless the patient is notified of these rights, they will not be effective. According to the *Mental Disability Law Reporter*, more than one-third of the states do make some provision to ensure that notice of rights is given to patients. Frequently a document is posted for reading in a location that is easily accessible to patients.[1] In some hospitals, the patient is given a listing of his rights on admission.

The Mental Health Systems Act (MHSA) was passed by Congress in 1980. It incorporated a patient's bill of rights in section 501.[2] In 1981, during the first months of the Reagan administration, the act was repealed; however, section 501 was retained. The act recommended, but did not mandate, that the bill of rights be included in state statutes, because some members of Congress thought that such laws were already in existence.[3]

However, in 1986 Congress did pass the Protection and Advocacy for Mentally Ill Individuals Act of 1986, which authorized the establishment of systems in each state to protect and advocate for the rights of the mentally ill.[4] Subsequently each state and territory designated a Protection and Advocacy

Agency for mentally ill individuals.

In 1982 a survey of state statutes was reported in the *Mental Disability Law Reporter*. It was found that "Only 22 states substantially complied with at least one-third of the act's major recommendations; only five states substantially complied with at least one-half (Alaska, 12; Montana, 13; Hawaii, 12; Illinois, 12; New York, 12)."[5] Adherence was greater in those sections not related to treatment, such as the right to receive visitors.

Another study, in 1985, investigated whether states had changed their laws based on the statutory language of section 501 of the MHSA. The results of this study indicated that there had not been an extensive effort to revise state laws. Thirteen states had amended their laws, and only Hawaii provided for most of the recommended rights.[6] The authors point out that lack of enforcement provisions severely limited the impact of the law. However, they emphasize that "...we believe that the *attitude* of concern with patients' rights among professionals and the public is much greater now than it was a few years ago."[7]

Civil Rights of Patients

Regardless of the differences in state law, it is particularly important to remember that unless a person has been declared incompetent prior to or at the time of admission to the facility, he maintains the civil rights of any citizen, such as the right to vote, to manage his financial affairs, and to execute legal documents.[8] As a result of the nature of the confinement of a patient in a mental health facility, he or she is guaranteed certain minimal legal rights. The right to consult or communicate with an attorney while hospitalized is considered to be constitutionally required. If the facility attempts to limit the right of a patient to have any visitors, including a lawyer, the position must be therapeutically defensible and well documented. One well-known expert in the field, Bruce Ennis, states that the only justification for denying this right "should be a compelling reason."[9]

Additionally, most states specify that a patient has the right to receive mail without interference or censorship, the right to receive visitors, and the right not to be denied the basic necessities of life in the name of treatment. Although these rights may be temporarily restricted under certain circumstances, a mere claim by the staff that interference with these rights is necessary for treatment purposes is insufficient to deny them to a patient.

One federal court stated that patients have a right to send and receive sealed mail from "attorneys, doctors, mental health professionals, and public officials."[10] Some states require that the patient "designate correspondents before communicating with them."[11] In *Davis v. Balson*, the court found the following practices unconstitutional in a maximum security hospital in Ohio: "the opening of incoming general correspondence outside the presence of the patient; the practice of reading and censoring outgoing mail from patients that have been the subject of complaints from members of the public."[12]

States vary in defining other legal rights. Almost half the states grant individuals the right to wear their personal clothes. Fewer than a quarter of the states delineate requirements for storage space for personal possessions.[13] Anyone who has visited a state hospital ward will have observed that privacy is difficult to obtain. Consequently, many states have passed legislation to ensure patients "some degree of personal privacy, autonomy, good health, and dignity."[14]

As stated in a previous chapter, confidentiality of the records of the mentally disabled is imperative. In addition, it is important to keep a complete and accurate record of the individual's course of treatment. Mental health professionals who have worked in state hospitals during the last 10 years cannot avoid noting the improvement in recordkeeping in regard to patients' course of treatment. This is probably due to the increase in the number of professionals working within the mental health system and the motivation of state systems to ensure that they receive accreditation by the Joint Commission on the Accreditation of Health Organizations.

Access to Patient Records

Approximately two-thirds of the states have passed statutes governing the accessibility of patient records.[15] Release forms should be signed by the patient or guardian before a professional disseminates information about the patient to anyone. Some community mental health centers are not part of the state hospital system; therefore, release forms should be obtained before sharing patient data with them. This should be accomplished in a timely manner so that continuity of patient care is maintained.

Review of Patient Records

Almost half the states require periodic review of the patient's condition to determine whether he continues to meet the standard for hospitalization.[16] Tennessee allows a patient to consult with a licensed physician practicing outside the hospital. If the person is indigent, the state system will provide the remuneration.[17] Since a person's condition is subject to change even after long periods of hospitalization, review of the patient's treatment plan should be routine. Ennis and Emergy propose that periodic judicial review be constitutionally required and recommends that judicial review of confined patients take place every six months.[18]

Least Restrictive Alternative

The concept of least restrictive alternative was discussed in Chapter 3 with emphasis on when to hospitalize a person. The concept applies within the hospital setting as well. During hospitalization, a change in a patient's condition may warrant a revision in the treatment plan; therefore, treatment regimens should be frequently evaluated. Mechanisms to transfer a client efficiently from one alternative to another should be developed.[19] Adequate documentation to justify the change should be present, particularly when the patient is being transferred to a more restrictive setting, because such a modification could be judicially reviewed.

Seclusion and Restraints

A substantial number of states have laws specifying and restricting the use of restraints and seclusion. The major guideline is that the restraint can be used only to prevent serious harm to the patient or to others in the immediate environment.[20] Seclusion practices were a major issue in the Massachusetts case of *Rogers v. Okin*. Although the court held that seclusion practices at Boston State Hospital had been utilized as a form of treatment and not as punishment, in some instances of isolation no "serious threat of extreme violence, personal injury, or attempted suicide" existed.[21] Therefore, seclusion should be based on whether the patient is harmful to himself or others. In the landmark case *Wyatt v. Stickney*, the court ruled:

> Patients have a right to be free from physical restraint and isolation. Except for emergency situations, in which it is likely that patients could harm themselves or others and in which less restrictive means of restraint are not feasible, patients may be physically restrained or placed in isolation only on a Qualified Mental Health Professional's written order which explains the rationale for such action. The written order may be entered only after the Qualified Mental Health Professional has person-

ally seen the patient concerned and evaluated whatever episode or situation is said to call for restraint or isolation. Emergency use of restraints or isolation shall be for no more than one hour, by which time a Qualified Mental Health Professional shall have been consulted and shall have entered an appropriate order in writing. Such written order shall be effective for no more than 24 hours and must be renewed if restraint and isolation are to be continued. While in restraint or isolation the patient must be seen by qualified ward personnel who will chart the patient's physical condition (if it is compromised) and psychiatric condition every hour. The patient must have bathroom privileges every hour and must be bathed every 12 hours.[22]

Several studies have looked at facets of seclusion and restraint. Okin studied admissions for seven state hospitals over a two-week period and followed individual patients until discharge for up to 16 weeks of hospitalization. The findings were that the hospitals operated under the same regulations for seclusion and restraint. However, the facilities used seclusion and restraint in varying patterns. The results demonstrated that practices varied greatly among institutions.[23]

Soloff and colleagues reviewed 13 studies of seclusion and restraint and also found that practices with regard to implementation of these procedures varied. The authors comment:

From a purely legalistic perspective, the wide disparity in seclusion times, and the lack of correlation between duration, precipitating behavior, and diagnosis raise unpleasant questions about arbitrary determination of duration of seclusion and its potential use as a punitive sanction. From the clinical perspective, staff or unit factors outside the individual patient's immediate needs may play a role in determining duration.[24]

Way looked at a sample of 2,150 orders for seclusion and restraint affecting 804 patients; the orders were written over a one-month period in 1984. The most frequent behaviors precipitating a seclusion or restraint order were assaulting a staff member (30%) and assaulting another patient (21%).[25] Most orders were written during the day shift (52%). Another study by nurses indicated that the usage of restraint was highest on the day shift. The authors point out that similar patient behaviors did not result in consistency in interventions by the health caregivers.[26]

The American Psychiatric Association task force on the psychiatric uses of seclusion and restraint stated the following indications for seclusion and restraint: to prevent harm to self or others when other methods have proved to be ineffective; to prevent damage to the physical environment and serious disarray of treatment programs; as part of a treatment plan for behavioral therapy; and to lessen stimulation to the patient.[27] Other recommendations include the following: Orders for restraint for seclusion should generally be valid for no more than 12 hours. The patient should be seen by the physician, who should examine the patient and document the justification for extending the patient's time in seclusion or restraints. Nursing staff should observe the patient visually every 15 minutes to evaluate his condition and should go into the room and directly observe the individual every two hours or less.[28]

Nursing Implications. Nurses should be familiar with the rules and regulations promulgated by the health care facility in which they work relating to seclusion and restraint of patients. Although it is sometimes necessary to seclude patients for their own and others' safety, this is an extraordinary deprivation of liberty. Documentation of the precipitating event that warranted seclusion, as well as alternatives attempted or considered, should be included in the patient's record. Recording of the patient's behavior during seclusion is important, including verbal interventions. The patient should be checked frequently, and continuing periods of seclusion should be carefully evaluated. Seclusion of patients has become a subject of litigation. The nurse should be forewarned that seclusion of patients must be therapeutically indicated and justified. It is suggested that a copy of the APA task force's guidelines on seclusion and restraint be obtained from the American Psychiatric Association.[29]

Inpatient Work

Several suits have been filed by patients concerning work performed in an institution. Some states provide for compensation at the minimum wage or higher.[30] The key element seems to be that patients should not be performing work that involves the continuing maintenance and operation of the hospital without remuneration. Ordinary tasks such as cleaning up around the patient's own bedside unit or housekeeping tasks on the ward do not require payment.[31]

In a consent order entered in *Schindenwolf v. Klein*, the following guideline was promulgated: "All work performed for which the institution should otherwise have to pay an employee shall be compensated."[32] The remuneration would have to be commensurate with that given to persons in the community, with the exception that it could be adjusted if the resident's disability inhibited his performance of the work.[33]

Payment for Hospitalization

Almost all jurisdictions require patients or their families to pay for the expense of hospitalization. This requirement pertains to voluntary as well as involuntary patients.[34] The specific statutory provisions in each state determine whether any person other than the patient can be held accountable for payment for care. Perlin writes, "Most modern cases have held that statutes imposing liability upon the estates of relatives of institutionalized mentally disabled persons for their care and maintenance are a legitimate exercise of legislative power." However, this view is not unanimous.[35] The following two cases upheld the right to exact payment. In Pennsylvania, parents of an incompetent 28-year-old man were required to pay the cost of his hospitalization in a state facility.[36] In another decision, an Oklahoma court concluded that collection of an unpaid $5,000 was recoverable from the estate of a patient.[37]

Right to Treatment

In 1970, a group of employees at Bryce Hospital in Tuscaloosa, Alabama, lost their jobs as a result of an impending deficit in the mental health department budget: "In October, 1971, a class action suit was filed in the United States District Court for the Middle District of Alabama on behalf of the employees and patients of Bryce Hospital; Ricky Wyatt, a patient on the adolescent unit and a relative of one of the employees, was named as plaintiff."[38]

The attorney for the plaintiffs set forth the premise that the dismissal of the employees would result in a lower standard of care and that patients had a constitutional right to treatment.[39] He acknowledged the contribution of a law student, who developed the idea based on a law review article which discussed the decision in *Rouse v. Cameron.*[40] That case involved an individual who was found not guilty by reason of insanity and was committed to a federal mental health facility. Judge David Bazelon ruled that institutionalized persons had a right to treatment, but this particular decision was based on a District of Columbia statute that delineated this right. Judge Frank M. Johnson, Jr., declined to hear the case related to the labor dispute but consented to consider the constitutional question of right to treatment.

In subsequent rulings, Judge Johnson stated that patients

did have a right to treatment. In one of the rulings concerning Bryce Hospital, he discussed the conditions at the facility. He commented that the "barnlike" dormitories afforded no privacy and that no space was set aside for individual patients to call their own. The admission procedure was demeaning and humiliating, and could cause a patient to form an impression of the hospital as a "prison or crazy house." Only 50 cents a day was spent on food for each patient, and the common sanitation procedure utilized at other hospitals was not followed at Bryce Hospital. It was a dehumanizing situation.[41] Some of the standards of care set forth by Judge Johnson for the operation of Bryce Hospital follow:

Patients have a right to privacy and dignity.

Patients have a right to the least restrictive conditions necessary to achieve the purposes of commitment.

Patients shall have the same rights to visitation and telephone communication as patients at other public hospitals, except to the extent that the Qualified Mental Health Professional responsible for formulation of a particular patient's treatment plan writes an order imposing special restrictions. The written order imposing special restrictions. The written order must be renewed after periodic review of the treatment plan if any restrictions are to be continued. Patients shall have an unrestricted right to visitation with attorneys and with private physicians and other health professionals.

Patients shall have an unrestricted right to send sealed mail. Patients shall have an unrestricted right to receive sealed mail from their attorneys, private physicians, and other mental health professionals, from courts, and government officials. Patients shall have a right to receive sealed mail from others, except to the extent that the Qualified Mental Health Professional responsible for formulation of a particular patient's treatment plan writes an order imposing special restrictions on receipt of sealed mail. The written order must be reviewed after each periodic review of the treatment plan if any restrictions are to be continued.

Patients have a right to wear their own clothes and use their own personal possessions except insofar as such clothes or personal possessions may be determined by a Qualified Mental Health Professional to be dangerous or otherwise inappropriate to the treatment regimen.

Each patient shall have a comprehensive physical and mental examination and review of behavioral status within 48 hours after admission to the hospital.

Each patient shall have an individualized treatment plan. The plan shall be developed by appropriate Qualified Mental Health Professionals, including a psychiatrist, and implemented as soon as possible—in any event no later than five days after the patient's admission. Each individualized treatment plan shall contain:

a. a statement of the nature of the specific problems and specific needs of the patient;

b. a statement of the least restrictive treatment conditions necessary to achieve the purposes of commitment;

c. a description of intermediate and long-range treatment goals, with a projected timetable for their attainment;

d. a statement and rationale for the plan of treatment for achieving these intermediate and long-range goals;

e.   a specification of staff responsibility and a description of proposed staff involvement with the patient in order to attain these treatment goals;

f.   criteria for release to less restrictive treatment conditions.[42]

Wyatt v. Stickney was subsequently upheld by the Fifth Circuit Court of Appeals in 1974.[43] Almost 10 years after the initial suit was filed, the state of Alabama was placed in receivership for failure to comply with the standards. The governor of Alabama was made receiver of the system, and a monitor was appointed to scrutinize compliance.[44]

Fifteen years after the initial litigation, *Wyatt v. Stickney* was settled with a consent decree in September 1986. The higher courts never "fully embraced" the right to treatment; however, the "Wyatt standards have not been specifically overruled."[45] Alabama never fully complied with the orders of the court, but the situation for patients has greatly improved. Court supervision can be reinstated if significant failure to comply with the settlement occurs. Stevens concludes that *Wyatt v. Stickney* ended with a whimper and that the current trend with the federal judiciary encourages settlement rather than judicial fact-finding.[46] The overall effect of this decision nationwide has been enormous. Flowing from this decision has been a phenomenal amount of litigation and legislation, which has markedly affected hospitalized patients' rights.[47]

In a U.S. Supreme Court case, *O'Connor v. Donaldson*, it was ruled that the state cannot hospitalize a nondangerous person in a mental institution against his will without treatment if he is capable of surviving safely in the community with a support system of friends and family.[48] Mr. Donaldson, diagnosed as paranoid schizophrenic, had been hospitalized for more than 14 years in a mental institution in Florida. After his first examination, Mr. Donaldson, a Christian Scientist, declined to

take medication or any other treatment, such as electroconvulsive therapy. He was confined in a locked room with about 60
other patients, one-third of whom were criminals. When Mr.
Donaldson asked for grounds privileges and occupational
therapy, his requests were rejected. One of his former college
classmates offered to take him into his home in New York State,
but these requests were denied by the hospital administration.
At no time was there evidence that Mr. Donaldson was in a
therapeutic milieu, although the hospital described it as such.
This premise was rejected by the court.[49] This was a very
limited decision and was not as encompassing a ruling as *Wyatt
v. Stickney*, which was a lower court decision that affects only
those states in the Fifth Circuit.

Another Supreme Court decision, *Youngberg v. Romeo*, also
ruled in a narrow fashion.[50] A mother filed a case against
Pennhurst State School and Hospital in Pennsylvania, alleging
that as a consequence of injuries to her profoundly retarded
adult son he was denied his constitutional rights. The court
ruled that under the due process clause of the Fourteenth
Amendment the son had constitutionally protected liberty
interests to

> reasonably safe conditions of confinement, freedom
> from unreasonable bodily restraints, and such mini-
> mally adequate training as reasonably may be required
> by these interests. Whether respondent's constitutional
> rights have been violated must be determined by bal-
> ancing these liberty interests against the relevant state
> interest. The proper standard for determining whether
> the State has adequately protected such right is whether
> professional judgment in fact was exercised. And in
> determining what is "reasonable," courts must show
> deference to the judgment exercised by a qualified
> professional, whose decision is presumptively valid.[51]

The patients in this institution were entitled to only that treatment that would enable them to remain free from unnecessary restraint and assault from others. Appelbaum writes, "Many advocates read the decision as an obituary for the right to treatment and the hopes it embodied."[52] This, however, has not proven to be true. In *Woe v. Cuomo*, the judge ruled:

Having undertaken to provide governmentally mandated care and treatment to involuntarily civilly committed patients, hospital administrators must provide constitutionally adequate treatment; they are not relieved of this responsibility by protesting that resources, either monetary or creative, are so scarce that inadequate care is preferable to no treatment at all.[53]

A class action suit was filed in Arizona in January 1985 on behalf of seriously mentally ill patients. In light of a successful adjudication by the judge, the Arizona legislators passed legislation mandating the creation of five pilot projects with prepaid funding to develop clinical teams to provide care. Each individual will be assigned a fixed amount of money depending on projected services utilization.[54]

The 1980 Civil Rights for Institutionalized Persons Act (CRIPA) allows the federal government through the Justice Department to bring actions against states "whose institutions deny residents (whether patients, prisoners, or others) their constitutional rights."[55] Consent decrees have been signed with several states, including South Carolina, Colorado, Connecticut, and Michigan. Terms of the agreements include specified staffing ratios, adequate health care, and improving the physical environment.[56]

Although the situation nationally with respect to institutional care for the mentally ill is not always ideal, there has generally been marked improvement in provision of care in those states with the worst deficiencies. The last two decades have wrought not only marked changes in the physical environment but also improvement in staffing ratios and the employment of more treatment personnel with advanced degrees and clinical certification.

Nursing Implications. Nurses can influence the care of patients in mental institutions by expressing their views through nursing organizations, influencing legislators at the state and the federal level, requesting consultation for an institution providing below-standard care, and developing suggested statewide plans for care.[57] Nurses make up the largest single group of professional health personnel. The power this implies has not been used to influence patient care as efficiently as could be expected by the sheer numbers. Nurses can use their energy and creativity to assist in formulating therapeutic programs to meet the needs of their patients. A well-conceived and implemented treatment plan that includes not only inpatient but aftercare planning has the potential to improve care. Every professional nurse should attend continuing education programs yearly in the specialty of choice, to insure that information about new ideas and treatments is heard. It is hoped that the chance to get away from the work environment and exchange ideas with other nurses and mental health caregivers will challenge nurses to try innovative approaches to care. It does not take long to become as discouraged and institutionalized as the patients themselves.

Behavioral Modification

Behavior therapies implemented for the treatment of the mentally ill and residents of prisons have varied widely. Most nurses are familiar with token economies, in which an individual can earn tokens or privileges by exhibiting positive behavior as outlined by the staff. Other, more intrusive methods have also been used in an attempt to change patients' behavior. The following case is an example.

In *Knecht v. Gillman,* residents of the Iowa Security Medical Facility filed suit alleging cruel and unusual punishment. This institution provided treatment for individuals who needed mental health services in a secure setting. The residents alleged that injections of apomorphine were given to them without consent and that this practice constituted cruel and unusual punishment, in violation of the Eighth Amendment. The drug was given as an aversive treatment to manage behavior problems. It was not clear whether or not informed consent was secured; however, if an inmate did consent to the procedure, later revocation of the consent was not permitted. A behavior protocol was established for the individual by the staff. Behaviors for which a resident could receive apomorphine included not getting up out of bed, giving cigarettes against orders, talking, swearing, and lying. Other inmates or staff would report breaches of the protocol, and a nurse would give the injection. The staff did not have to observe the violation themselves for the medication to be given.

After the hypodermic injection was given, the individual was made to exercise for 15 minutes until he began vomiting. Vomiting usually continued for 15 minutes to an hour. The physiologic changes associated with administration of apomorphine include changes in blood pressure and in functioning of the heart. The court, after reviewing the facts, stated that forcing an individual to vomit for a minor infraction of the rules could only be regarded as cruel and unusual punishment, unless the person "knowingly and intelligently has consented to it."[58] The court issued the following rules: If the procedure was to continue, written consent and certification by a physician was necessary, and the patient must know and understand all the terms of the agreement. The consent could be revoked at any time. Each injection had to be authorized by a physician and administered by a doctor or nurse. The staff had to observe personally the unacceptable behavior that could result in administration of the medication.

Even though the court ruled that this procedure could be utilized with these specific guidelines, one might question whether this form of behavior modification should be considered as a possible treatment. Rosoff comments on the coercive atmosphere of this situation.[59]

In another case, a licensed practical nurse (LPN) was employed by a special education center caring for orthopedically handicapped adults and children. In 1984, the nurse and an aide placed a 12-year-old, who was "screaming, hollering, and crying," into a bathtub and sprayed the child twice with cold water. The LPN did not consult with a registered nurse prior to this event. The policy of the institution was that a disruptive client was to be removed to an observation room and the behavior was to be ignored. If injury to others or property damage was imminent, the client was to be seated between the employee's knees and the shoulders were to be held. Because of this incident and several other events for which she was counseled, the nurse was dismissed from her employment. She filed suit to protest her termination. The court found that the "appellant chose to disregard the instructions and to institute an independent and unsanctioned program of behavior modification." The decision was upheld by the Court of Appeals in Louisiana.[60]

Nursing Implications. To ensure that a patient's rights are not violated, it is important to be familiar with institutional or departmental guidelines. The more intrusive the procedure, the greater the need for informed consent. Martin sets forth comprehensive checklists that would be useful to review before starting such a program.[61] These include questions to be addressed before obtaining informed consent; goal setting; effectiveness evaluation; supervision and control; and written documentation.

Research on the Mentally Ill

Institutional review boards (IRB) were created by the federal government to prevent violation of patients' rights for projects funded by the federal government. Many institutions adopted guidelines permitting the review boards to peruse all research that utilized human subjects, even projects not funded by the federal government. The major thrust of the guidelines is to ensure informed consent, and to guarantee that any risks to the patient are outweighed by the potential benefits. The knowledge to be gained from the project should warrant allowing the subject to accept the risks.[62]

The following are guidelines established by the federal government for research. Each subject should receive the following information.

(1) A statement that the study involves research, an explanation of the purposes of the research and the expected duration of the subject's participation, a description of the procedures to be followed, and identification of any procedures which are experimental;

(2) A description of any reasonably foreseeable risks or discomforts to the subject;

(3) A description of any benefits to the subject or to others which may reasonably be expected from the research;

(4) A disclosure of appropriate alternative procedures or courses of treatment, if any, that might be advantageous to the subject;

(5) A statement describing the extent, if any, to which confidentiality of records identifying the subject will be maintained;

(6) For research involving more than minimal risk, an explanation as to whether any compensation and an explanation as to whether any medical treatments are available if injury occurs and, if so, what they consist of, or where further information may be obtained;

(7) An explanation of whom to contact for answers to pertinent questions about the research and research subjects' rights, and whom to contact in the event of a research-related injury to the subject; and

(8) A statement that participation is voluntary, refusal to participate will involve no penalty or loss of benefits to which the subject is otherwise entitled, and the subject may discontinue participation at any time without penalty or loss of benefits to which the subject is otherwise entitled.

Additional elements of informed consent. When appropriate, one or more of the following elements of information shall also be provided to each subject:

(1) A statement that the particular treatment or procedure may involve risks to the subject (or to the embryo or fetus, if the subject is or may become pregnant) which are currently unforeseeable;

(2) Anticipated circumstances under which the subject's participation may be terminated by the investigator without regard to the subject's consent;

(3) Any additional costs to the subject that may result from participation in the research;

(4) The consequences of a subject's decision to withdraw from the research and procedures for orderly termination of participation by the subject;

(5) A statement that significant new findings developed during the course of the research which may relate to the subject's willingness to continue participation will be provided to the subject; and

(6) The approximate number of subjects involved in the study.[63]

In 1978, the National Commission for the Protection of Human Subjects of Biomedical and Behavior Research developed some recommendations for research involving the mentally infirm who are institutionalized.[64] These recommendations were never implemented because researchers expressed the view that this population was no different from individuals with serious medical problems and that limitations would impede research.[65] Special guidelines have been issued by the U.S. Department of Health and Human Services for especially vulnerable populations. These groups are pregnant women, fetuses, products of in vitro fertilization, children, and inmates in prisons.[66]

Nursing Implications. It is important for nurses working on units where research is being conducted to be certain that the researchers have gone through the proper channels to have the research approved. It is also imperative that nurse researchers be cognizant of the procedure for approval of research within their own institution as well as within the agency or facility in which they plan to conduct the research.

Social Security

Certain groups of the mentally ill are eligible for Social Security benefits as a result of their disability. In 1981, a new federal administration instigated an initiative to save funds through a cutback on Social Security Disability Insurance (SSDI) disbursements. A review of cases was conducted to validate whether the "truly disabled" were receiving benefits.[67] Goldman and Gattozzi state that one in four of those dropped from the rolls was mentally disabled, although overall only one in nine beneficiaries was mentally ill. According to Goldman and Gattozzi:

> Hundreds of thousands of mentally or physically impaired persons were eliminated from the SSDI and SSI rolls, a large portion unfairly, and scores of suicides and early deaths were documented before the situation was substantially eased in June, 1983. The Secretary of Health and Human Services exempted two-thirds of the mentally impaired beneficiaries to avert "hardships and heartbreaks."[68]

Nursing Implications. Some mentally ill individuals find it difficult to return to work for any length of time because of the symptomatology of their illness. Although nursing is usually not involved in the obtaining of funding for patients, in some community mental health facilities the nurse may be totally responsible for assisting the patient in contacting a Social Security office. Although mental illness per se does not entitle a person to compensation, those individuals who find it difficult to pursue employment for sustained periods of time may be eligible.

Right to Aftercare

Many articles have been written in the professional and the lay literature about some of the deplorable conditions faced by deinstitutionalized mental patients upon leaving the hospital. Titles of articles vividly depict the situation: "Out of Their Beds and Into the Streets" and "Health Care's Dumping Ground" characterize the plight of the chronically mentally disabled in the community.[69] One author describes some former mental patients as "ragtag figures seen huddled in doorways."[70] In 1977, public hearings were held across the country by the President's Commission on Mental Health. During these sessions, individuals testified to the lack of aftercare services and the fragmentation of care.

Reports have indicated that only 10% to 30% of discharged mental hospital patients acquire employment; exacerbations of the illness and rehospitalization rates range from 35% to 50% in the first year after discharge, and from 65% to 75% within five years.[71] Fragmentation and disorganization of service delivery are frequently mentioned as causes. Lamb recommends that a variety of community living arrangements be established and given financial support. This will not be inexpensive, but unless the underfunding of programs ceases, "We will continue to provide deplorable conditions for our severely mentally ill, and the 'shame of the states' will simply have been moved to the community."[72]

The above paragraphs were written in 1983. The situation for the homeless mentally ill has not changed since then except that the situation has become possibly more acute.

Joyce Brown came from a middle-class New Jersey family and worked for 10 years as a secretary. In 1985 she was given psychotropic medication and discharged from a mental health facility. She went to live on the streets of New York City. She was brought to emergency rooms on three different occasions but was not admitted. In October 1987, she was removed from the street by Project HELP and admitted to a hospital psychiatric unit. She filed a petition for release with the assistance of lawyers from the American Civil Liberties Union. The psychiatrists who examined her could not agree on whether she needed to be hospitalized. The hospital psychiatrist found her to be "delusional, suicidal, and unable to make competent decisions." The defense psychiatrists found her to be coherent and logical; however, the psychiatrists examined her at different times. Because of the inconsistent testimony, the court assessed her demeanor and behavior in the courtroom.

The court concluded that Ms. Brown was not suicidal or homicidal, but that there was a serious question about her ability to meet her essential needs. The court could not find clear and convincing evidence of dangerousness. On January 15, 1988, the trial court denied the request to medicate Ms. Brown, and she was discharged four days later.

An intermediate New York appeals court reversed the lower court decision, stating there was clear and convincing evidence that Ms. Brown was mentally ill and needed to be hospitalized. The appeals court was impressed with evidence from a psychiatrist and a psychiatric social worker who had observed her behavior on the street, which included screaming at passers by and urinating and defecating in the streets. Her behavior in court was more appropriate, as she had recently received a week's hospital treatment.[73]

Talbott and Lamb write that the homeless mentally ill need "supervised settings, access to care, and nonintrusive but humane monitoring."[74] They argue that, "even though legal advocates contend 'liberty is more important than treatment,'...we must choose between humane treatment of impaired persons at an increased cost to society or continuing inhumanity toward those who cannot fend for themselves."[75]

In *Dixon v. Weinberger*, the court stated that patients should be placed in the least restrictive alternative, and that solutions to the problems of placing patients in these situations must be submitted.[76] This case has spanned two decades, and in *Dixon v. Bowen* goals and objectives for making progress to move residents from institutions were negotiated.[77]

A consent decree in *Brewster v. Dukakis* stipulated "that community programs would have to be upgraded, and alternatives created where none existed."[78] Saphire contends in a law review article that aftercare is a constitutional right. This issue has not been ruled upon by the courts, but all mental health professionals should attempt to provide continuity of care as well as adequate planning for the patient's continued care upon discharge from the hospital.[79]

Nursing Implications. Nurses should make every attempt in conjunction with the therapeutic team to ensure that follow-up plans are conceived before a patient's discharge. Some states have adopted a policy that mental health center staff should continue to be in contact with hospitalized patients. Nurses working in community settings should follow up on chronically mentally ill clients who fail to keep their appointments.

Advocacy

Some states have developed advocacy projects within mental health facilities in their system. The purpose of advocacy is not only to ensure that the legal rights of patients are protected, but also to improve the quality of the day-to-day life of patients in the institutional setting. The MHSA of 1980 originally provided federal support for such programs, but this law was repealed.[80] Advocates assist patients in maintaining their rights. Kopolow states that patients have "the right not to be psychiatric patients" and that patients today are more likely to assert their rights and less apt to be passive recipients of care.[81] Many patients' rights groups organized in the last 10 years throughout the country are currently setting forth their views on mental health care. The National Alliance for the Mentally Ill has been influencing the earmarking of funds for research.

In a survey conducted in California, 199 respondents of the California Alliance for the Mentally Ill indicated their concerns for family members with a mental disability. They designated support of the family, medication, socialization centers, and community residential treatment as well as locked facilities as assisting the family in relating to the disabled relative. Unmet needs included "housing, vocational and social opportunities and research."[82]

In Maryland, a consent decree allowed for an internal grievance procedure and a legal advocacy system, which was contracted out to a mental health law group. These advocates have access to patients to assist them not only in areas related to their mental health condition but also in such matters as landlord and tenant problems. Appelbaum discloses that the consent decree

> stirred up a good deal of resentment among clinicians in Maryland, who were locked out of the negotiation process and presented with the decree as a *fait accompli*. Their fears over the disruption of clinical care and their personal liability have been exacerbated both by the reportedly intemperate behavior of some of the legal advocates and by the failure of the state of Maryland to guarantee payment of their legal expenses and judgments resulting from suits.[83]

Written statements regarding patients' rights may have a limited impact on the life of the patient or the quality of care provided him. At least three areas of advocacy can be identified that would maximize the fulfillment of patients' rights: (1) to educate and train the facility staff properly and to implement policies and procedures that recognize and protect patients' rights; (2) to establish an additional procedure to permit the speedy resolution of problems, questions, or disagreements that occur and that may or may not be based on legal rights; and (3) to provide access to legal services when a patient's legal rights have been denied. The third area usually requires an advocate who is not employed by the facility but is located at the facility.

Under the Protection and Advocacy for Mentally Ill Individuals Act of 1986, all states must designate an agency which is responsible for protecting the rights of the mentally ill. The agency designated may vary depending on the state. In

Tennessee, Effective Advocacy for Citizens with Handicaps, Inc. (E.A.C.H., Inc.), is a private nonprofit volunteer membership organization, whereas in Texas, Advocacy, Inc., is appointed to represent clients.

Although many mental health professionals applaud the advocacy movement, one author has expressed concern about advocates who create a situation in which the mental health professional and the advocate are placed in an adversary position for long periods, leading to mutual suspicion and subsequent poor and fragmented care. Lamp suggests that advocates should be required to receive in-depth education concerning the nature of mental illness. Following this educational experience, direct service should be provided by the advocates to very disturbed patients within a psychiatric facility.[84] This would give the advocates perspective on the treatment of psychiatric patients. Some might argue, however, that advocates would lose their objectivity if this process took place routinely.

The role of advocates within a mental health care system should be carefully outlined by administrators to avoid confusion among the staff giving care. Kopolow recommends that psychiatrists advocate treatment alternatives to hospitalization and support changes in the laws when needed.[85] For nurses who have traditionally attempted to ensure that patients are granted their rights, careful thought must be given to the delivery of nursing care and to advocating changes that would allow improvement of care.

Nursing Implications. Nurses should be aware of the basic rights of mental health patients as established within the mental health care system. If certain basic rights are delineated in statutes or outlined in case law, mechanisms should be put in place within a health care facility to guarantee those rights. If a nurse observes a violation of a patient's rights, the incident should be reported to an administrator. Nurses must stay informed through continuing education programs and by reading material that outlines legislative and judicial changes in the law. Because of the large number of registered professional nurses in each state, political power bases for influencing passage of legislation that guarantees protection of patients' rights can be established.

References

1. Rights of Disabled Persons in Residential Facilities. *Mental Disability Law Reporter*, 3, no. 5, 1979, pp. 348–365.
2. Mental Health Systems Act of 1980. Pub. L. no. 96–398, 94 Stat 1564 (1980).
3. Martha Lyon, Martin Levine and Jack Susman: Patient Bill of Rights: A Survey of State Statutes. *Mental Disability Law Reporter*, 6, no. 3, May-June 1982, pp. 178–199.
4. Pub. L. 99-319, 100 Stat 485 (1986).
5. Lyon, Levine and Susman: Patient Bill of Rights, p. 179.
6. Martha Lyon-Levine, Martin Levine and Jack Zusman: Developments in Patients' Bill of Rights Since the Mental Health Systems Act. *Mental and Physical Disability Law Reporter*, 9, no. 2, March-April 1985, pp. 146–152.
7. Ibid., p. 153.
8. Rights of Disabled Persons in Residential Facilities, pp. 348–365.
9. Bruce Ennis and Richard D. Emery: *The Rights of Mental Patients, An American Civil Liberties Union Handbook*, New York, Avon Books, 1978, p. 154.
10. *Wyatt v. Stickney*, 344 F. Supp. 373 (1972), at 379.
11. Rights of Disabled Persons in Residential Facilities, p. 349.
12. *Davis v. Balson*, 461 F.Supp. 842 (W.D. Ohio, 1978).
13. Rights of Disabled Persons in Residential Facilities, p. 348.
14. Ibid.
15. Ibid.
16. Ibid., pp. 357–359.
17. *Tennessee Code Annotated*, 33-6-108(b)(1).
18. Ennis and Emery: *The Rights of Mental Patients*, p. 128.
19. Reed Martin: Workshop Materials. In *Legal Challenges in Regulating Behavior Change*. Champaign, Ill., Research Press Co., Public Law Div., 1979, p. 27.

20. Rights of Disabled Persons in Residential Facilities, p. 348.
21. *Rogers v. Okin*, 478 F.Supp. 1342 (D. Mass. 1979), at 1374. See also *Rogers v. Okin*, 634 F.2d 650 (1st Cir. 1980).
22. *Wyatt v. Stickney*, 344 F.Supp. 373 (1972), at 380.
23. Robert Okin: Variation Among State Hospitals in Use of Seclusion and Restraint. *Hospital and Community Psychiatry*, 36, no. 6, June 1986, pp. 648–652.
24. Paul Soloff, Thomas Gutheil and David Wexler: Seclusion and Restraint in 1985: A Review and Update. *Hospital and Community Psychiatry*, 36, no. 6, June 1985, pp. 652–657, at 656.
25. Bruce Way: The Use of Restraint and Seclusion in New York State Psychiatric Centers. *International Journal of Law and Psychiatry*, 8, 1986, pp. 383–393.
26. Janice Roper, Adam Coutts, Janet Suther and Rosella Taylor: Restraint and Seclusion. *Journal of Psychosocial Nursing and Mental Health Services*, 23, no. 6, June 1985, pp. 18–23.
27. APA Task Force Issues Guidelines for Use of Seclusion and Restraint in Inpatient Settings. *Hospital and Community Psychiatry*, 36, no. 6, June 1985, pp. 677–679.
28. Ibid.
29. Ibid.
30. Rights of Disabled Persons in Residential Facilities, pp. 360–362.
31. California Patient Labor Case Settled. *Mental Disability Law Reporter*, 5, no. 3, 1981, p. 187.
32. Expansive Work Program Outlined for New Jersey Psychiatric Patients. *Mental Disability Law Reporter*, 5, no. 1, 1981, pp. 60–63.
33. Ibid.
34. Ennis and Emery: *The Rights of Mental Patients*, p. 156.
35. Michael Perlin: Economic Rights of the Institutionalized Mentally Disabled. *International Journal of Law and Psychiatry*, 10, pp. 187–214, 1987, at 196.
36. *Lansing v. Pennsylvania Department of Public Welfare*, 410 A.2d 982 (Pa. 1980).
37. *Oklahoma v. Storer*, 614 P.2d 59 (Okla. 1980).
38. *Wyatt v. Stickney*: Retrospect and Prospect. *Hospital and Community Psychiatry*, 32, no. 2, February 1981, pp. 123–126, at 124.
39. Carole W. Offir: Civil Rights and the Mentally Ill:Revolution in Bedlam. *Psychology Today*, October 1974, p. 61.
40. *Rouse v. Cameron*, 373 F.2d 451 (D.C. Cir. 1957).

41. *Wyatt v. Stickney*, 334 F.Supp. 1341 (1971), at 1343.
42. *Wyatt v. Stickney*, 344 F.Supp. 373, 379, 384 (1972).
43. *Wyatt v. Aderholt*, 503 F.2d 1305 (5th Cir. 1974).
44. *Wyatt v. Stickney*: Retrospect and Prospect, p. 125.
45. Edward Stevens: *Wyatt v. Stickney* Concludes with a Whimper. *Mental and Physical Disability Law Reporter*, 11, no. 2, March-April 1987, pp. 134–140, at 139.
46. Ibid.
47. Harry C. Schnibne: How the States Have Met the Challenge, "10 Years After." Paper presented at a symposium on the *Wyatt v. Stickney* case, Tuscaloosa, Ala., September 25–26, 1980.
48. *O'Connor v. Donaldson*, 422 U.S. 563 (1975).
49. *Donaldson v. O'Connor*, 493 F.2d 507 (5th Cir. 1974).
50. *Youngberg v. Romeo*, 457 U.S. 308 (1982).
51. Ibid.
52. Paul Appelbaum: Resurrecting the Right to Treatment. *Hospital and Community Psychiatry*, 38, no. 7, July 1987, pp. 703–704, 721, at 703.
53. *Woe v. Cuomo*, 638 F.Supp. 1506 (E.D. N.Y. 1986), at 1507.
54. Jose M. Santiago: Reforming a System of Care: The Arizona Experiment. *Hospital and Community Psychiatry*, 38, no. 3, March 1987, pp. 270–273.
55. Resurrecting the Right to Treatment, p. 704.
56. Justice Department Consent Decree. *Mental and Physical Disability Law Reporter*, 10, no. 4, July-August 1986, p. 285. Justice Department CRIPA Actions. *Mental and Physical Disability Law Reporter*, 10, no. 5, September-October 1986, pp. 355–356.
57. Joyce Laben and Lona Spencer: Decentralization of Forensic Services. *Community Mental Health Journal*, 12, no. 4, 1976, pp. 405–414.
58. *Knecht v. Gillman*, 488 F.2d 1136 (8th Cir. 1973), at 1139.
59. Arnold J. Rosoff: *Informed Consent*. Rockville, Md., Aspen Systems Corp., 1981, p. 234.
60. *Juneau v. Louisiana Board of Elementary and Secondary Education*, 506 So.2d 756 (La. App. 1st Cir. 1987), at 759.
61. Martin: Workshop Materials, pp. 110–115.
62. George J. Annas, Leonard H. Glantz and Barbara F. Katz: *The Rights of Doctors, Nurses and Allied Health Professionals*. New York, Avon Books, 1981, p. 142.

63. 45 *Code of Federal Regulations Section 46.116.*

64. Protection of Human Subjects. Research Involving Those Institutionalized as Mentally Infirm; Report and Recommendations for Public Comment. *Federal Register*, 43, pp. 11328–11358.

65. Paul Appelbaum, Charles Lidz and Alan Meisal: *Informed Consent. Legal Theory and Clinical Practice*, New York, Oxford University Press, 1987, p. 228.

66. Ibid.

67. Howard Goldman and Antoinette Gattozzi: Murder in the Cathedral Revisited: President and the Mentally Disabled. *Hospital and Community Psychiatry*, 39, no. 3, March 1988, pp. 505–509.

68. Ibid., p. 506.

69. Henry Santiestevan: *Out of Their Beds and Into the Streets*, Washington, D.C., American Federation of State and County Employees, December 1976. See also Samantha G. Johnson: Health Care's Dumping Ground. *The Boston Globe Magazine*, May 30, 1982, pp. 7, 14, 16–20.

70. Johnson: Health Care's Dumping Ground, p. 14.

71. W. A. Anthony, M. R. Cohen and R. Vitulo: The Measurement of Rehabilitation Outcome. *Schizophrenia Bulletin*, 4, no. 3, 1978, pp. 365-383. See also H. Richard Lamb: What Did We Really Expect from Deinstitutionalization? *Hospital and Community Psychiatry*, 32, no. 2, February 1981, pp. 105–109.

72. Lamb: What Did We Really Expect, p. 109.

73. Helpless Woman Released from New York Hospital. *Mental and Physical Disability Law Reporter*, 12, no. 1, January-February 1988, pp. 14–15. New York Court Reverses Release of Homeless Woman. *Mental and Physical Disability Law Reporter*, 12, no. 3, May-June 1988, pp. 238–239.

74. John Talbott and H. Richard Lamb: The Homeless Mentally Ill. *Archives of Psychiatric Nursing*, 1, no. 6, 1987, pp. 379–384, at 381.

75. Ibid., p. 383.

76. *Dixon v. Weinberger*, 405 F.Supp. 974 (D.C. 1975).

77. John Parry: 1987 in Review. *Mental and Physical Disability Law Reporter*, 12, no. 1, January-February 1988, pp. 2–9, at 8.

78. Martin: Workshop Materials, p. 131.

79. Richard B. Saphire: The Civilly-Committed Public Mental Patient and the Right to Aftercare. *Florida State University Law Review*, 4, 1975, pp. 232–295.

80. Mental Health Systems Act of 1980, Publ. No. 93–398, 94 Stat 1564 (1980).
81. Louis E. Kopolow: Consumer Demands in Mental Health Care. *International Journal of Law and Psychiatry*, 2, 1979, pp. 263–270, at 269.
82. Patricia William, William A. Williams, Robert Sommer and Barbara Sommer: A Survery of the California Alliance for the Mentally Ill. *Hospital and Community Psychiatry*, 37, no. 3, 1986, pp. 253–256, at 253.
83. Paul Appelbaum: The Rising Tide of Patient Rights Advocacy. *Hospital and Community Psychiatry*, 37, no. 1, January 1986, pp. 9–10.
84. Richard Lamb: Securing Patient's Rights—Responsibly. *Hospital and Community Psychiatry*, 32, no. 6, June 1981, pp. 393–397.
85. Kopolow: Consumer Demands, pp. 263–270.

CHAPTER 5

The Right to Refuse Treatment

In recent years there has been a proliferation of lawsuits concerning the right to refuse treatment, especially treatment involving psychotropic drugs. Many states have guidelines for the administration of electroconvulsive therapy (ECT) and psychosurgery; however, the controversy over refusal of medication is a more recent occurrence.

ECT and psychosurgery are performed by physicians, with nurses sometimes assisting; however, nurses should be informed about recent court decisions relating to pharmacotherapy because they are primarily responsible for the actual administration of medications. Administration of psychotropic medication is problematic because the U.S. Supreme Court has not resolved the issue of whether it can be administered involuntarily, and some state statutes permit the involuntary administration of medication. The nurse probably will be the first person confronted with the patient's refusal of medication. This chapter discusses several cases related to medication refusal and the concerns that surround the issue.

Rennie v. Klein

John Rennie, an involuntary patient at Ancora Psychiatric Hospital in New Jersey, filed a complaint in December 1977 seeking an injunction (an order to stop) to enjoin the psychiatrists and officials at Ancora from forcibly medicating him without a presenting emergency situation.[1] Mr. Rennie, a highly intelligent former pilot and flight instructor, had a history of many hospitalizations in public and private facilities beginning in 1973 after the death of his twin brother in an airplane accident.

During Mr. Rennie's confinement in the hospital, physicians had been unable to arrive at a precise diagnosis of his condition. Some doctors identified a schizophrenic process; others concluded that he suffered from manic depression. There was likewise no consensus concerning the appropriate medication to be given to him.

Symptoms exhibited during his illness included delusions, aggressive behavior with homicidal threats, and suicidal gestures. During the admission that prompted the initial lawsuit, he was placed in a unit described as a "barren, bleak ward."[2] He had long periods of unproductive, unplanned time and infrequent contact with physicians, although such contact increased after the lawsuit was filed. Before the lawsuit, even though his condition had been deteriorating, he still refused to take medication. After the facility consulted with and was granted permission by the New Jersey Attorney General's office, he was given medication without his consent. Injectable fluphenazine (Prolixin) was selected because of its long-lasting effect; the need for administration was once every two weeks. It was considered an ideal treatment modality because of Mr. Rennie's previous noncompliance with medication regimens upon discharge. Subsequently he filed the lawsuit and the request for an injunction.

Mr. Rennie developed side effects from chlorpromazine (Thorazine) or Prolixin. He suffered from akathisia (an inability to be still), uncontrollable tremors, and wormlike movements of the tongue, which might have indicated the presence of tardive dyskinesia, prominent symptoms of which are "face and neck movements including chewing, smacking and licking of the lips, sucking, tongue protrusions, tongue tremor with open mouth, wormlike movements on the surface of the tongue, blinking, and facial distortions."[3] The prevalence of this condition has been reported to be between 10% and 20% of patients receiving antipsychotic medication, although some reports indicate a higher percentage.[4] The condition "has been found to be irreversible in some patients."[5] For these reasons, Mr. Rennie did not want to take the medication.

The court ruled on the basis of the right of privacy that mental patients in nonemergency situations could refuse treatment. However, it is a qualified right, taking into account the patient's threat of physical harm to other persons, the patient's capacity to make decisions for himself, the existence and availability of less restrictive treatment, and the risk of permanent side effects.

Because Mr. Rennie was no longer receiving involuntary administration of Prolixin, an injunction was not issued at the time of the first court hearing. Later, in 1978, Mr. Rennie returned to court again seeking an injunction, this time to halt the administration of Thorazine against his will. In an opinion issued in December 1978, the court decided, on the basis of his current behavior, that Mr. Rennie did not have the capacity to make decisions concerning the intake of drugs and that the least restrictive treatment at that time was medication.[6]

In 1979, Mr. Rennie filed another lawsuit for injunctive relief against hospitals and staff to prevent the forcible administration of drugs. The lawsuit was expanded to a class action which included persons currently hospitalized or who might be hospitalized in the future at Ancora Psychiatric Hospital, involuntarily committed patients of the five mental health facilities operated by the Division of Mental Health and Hospitals in New Jersey, and voluntary patients residing in the five facilities.[7]

A procedure had been outlined in an administrative bulletin issued in March 1978 by the Division of Mental Health

Hospitals for handling patients who refused to take prescribed medication. Under this procedure, voluntary patients had a right to refuse medication. However, if an involuntary patient refused, the physician was required first to inform the patient about his condition and then to describe the risks and benefits of the drugs to be given, including any other available alternative treatments. If the patient still refused, the treatment team was to review the issue. The team included nurses, social workers, psychologists, and the treating physician. The finding of the team was presented only as a recommendation to the treating physician, who had the ultimate responsibility for prescribing drugs.

Patients who were legally competent could have their cases reviewed by the medical director of the hospital. Before authorizing the involuntary administration of medication, the medical director was required to conduct a personal examination of the patient. An independent psychiatrist could be consulted if desired. The medical director was then required to review the treatment program of the patient each week that the patient protested the administration of involuntary medication. The patient could request that an attorney be present during this process.

If a patient found incompetent by the court refused medication, the guardian would be consulted. If the treatment team disagreed with the physician, either the medical director or his designee would examine the patient. If this physician agreed with the prior opinions, consent of the guardian would again be sought. If the guardian did not consent, the chief executive officer could consent.

In March 1979, an additional review procedure was added. Physicians in the central office of the Division of Mental Health and Hospitals were authorized to review further authorization of the use of involuntary medication. At the time of the hearing, only two patients' records, including that of Mr. Rennie, had been reviewed. The court found that this was not a regular procedure that patients could trust.

In making its decision, the court relied on examples of several patients and their refusals to take medications. One example was a 23-year-old female patient who testified in the case and whose demeanor impressed the judge. While a patient, she became pregnant and openly resisted taking medication because she did not want to harm the baby.[8] The physician continued to prescribe haloperidol (Haldol), a psychotropic drug. The patient complained to the public advocate's office, which interceded, but the hospital medical director did not change the order. Subsequently, she ingested some detergent and was transferred to the medical unit of the hospital. The drug was then discontinued because her diagnosis did not warrant the use of psychotropics. She began to do small chores on the ward, and her condition improved to the extent that she was discharged two months after admission to the medical unit.[9]

After hearing the evidence in the case, the federal district court ruled that patients had constitutional rights of privacy and due process while involuntarily committed. The court further held that the following procedures, which apply to psychotropic medication only, should be adopted. All patients, voluntary or involuntary, have to sign consent forms to be used in all nonemergency situations, except when the patient has been declared legally or functionally incompetent. (The term "legally incompetent" indicates that a court has adjudicated that the individual is unable to manage his affairs; "functionally incompetent" means that a physician has determined that the individual cannot make a medication decision for himself.) The forms must contain information about the drugs and their side effects. Also, patient advocates would be required to analyze those cases in which patients were considered incompetent to make an informed decision about their medication. The advocate could enlist in-hospital and independent review of the medication order. Advocates could also serve as informal counsel to patients who refused their medications.

An informal review by an independent psychiatrist would be required before the hospital could forcibly medicate an involuntary patient. It was the belief of the court that a psychiatrist would be more effective than a judge, an attorney, or a layperson. During an emergency situation, both voluntary and involuntary patients could be medicated to prevent harm.

> The court holds that the qualified privacy right is always outweighed in these emergency situations where the patient is in an acute psychotic state, has little competence but often is in great need of a psychotropic drug, and short-term use presents very little risk of permanent side effects.[10]

The New Jersey State Hospital officials appealed the decision. In 1981, the U.S. Third Circuit Court of Appeals ruled that the administration of psychotropic medication to involuntarily committed patients not adjudicated incompetent must be determined to be the least restrictive means of treatment. The court, however, stated that it was not necessary to have an adversary hearing before an independent psychiatrist, as outlined by the federal court judge. The court further held that the procedures instituted by the Division of Mental Health and Hospitals did satisfy due process.

Rennie v. Klein was appealed and was reviewed by the U.S. Supreme Court in a one-sentence opinion, and was remanded to the Third Circuit Court of Appeals in light of the recent decision *Youngberg v. Romeo.* Although the *Youngberg* case involved issues related to the institutionalization of a mentally retarded individual, the Supreme Court opinion analyzed certain rights of institutionalized persons that could be applied to the mentally ill as well. The court refused to rule on whether or not a right to minimally adequate habilitation existed, but it recognized that if habilitation was necessary in order to protect the person's safety and freedom from restraints, it was constitutionally required. The Supreme Court applied the standard that professionals' judgment would be deferred to unless they had departed so substantially from the standards and accepted professional judgment "as to demonstrate that the person responsible actually did not base the decision on such a judgment."[11] After the case was remanded back to the Third Circuit Court of Appeals, the court sitting *en banc* split its decision, with five judges rejecting utilization of the least restrictive alternative principle for short-term administration of drugs; four would apply the principle, and one did not discuss it specifically.[12] The state of New Jersey continues to use an administrative procedure for administering medication to refusing patients.

Rogers v. Okin

Rogers v. Okin was initially filed in April 1975 as a class action civil rights suit under a federal statute.[13] In this action, the plaintiffs sought to enjoin Boston State Hospital in Massachusetts from specific seclusion and medication practices, and monetary damages were sought. The class action suit was brought by seven patients involuntarily committed to Boston State Hospital against the Commissioner of Mental Health, 13 physicians, and one individual with a doctorate in counseling. The alleged grievance was forcing patients to submit to medication and seclusion in violation of state and federal law. A temporary restraining order was issued in April 1975 prohibiting nonemergency seclusion and involuntary medication of voluntary and involuntary patients. If a person was adjudicated incompetent, the guardian could give consent.

After many motions, the trial began in December 1977; it involved 72 trial days. The opinion of the federal district court was issued on October 29, 1979. Judge Tauro ruled that patients had been secluded in nonemergency situations in violation of the state statute that provided for seclusion only in emergency situations "where there is the occurrence of [or] serious threat of extreme violence, personal injury or attempted suicide."[14]

The major controversy, however, centered on the issue of a patient's right to refuse forced medications. The defendants presented the argument that involuntarily committed patients should automatically be considered incompetent when refusing medication. The court rejected this premise and ruled that a patient was presumed to be legally competent to make treatment decisions unless he had been specifically adjudicated otherwise. An involuntary patient who refused medication could only be forced to take drugs if a legally appointed guardian consented to their administration or if an emergency situation existed. Voluntary patients had a right to refuse treatment, and the only instance in which they could be medicated against their will was an emergency situation in which substantial likelihood of physical harm to the patient or others existed.[15]

The court based the right to refuse treatment on an individual's right to privacy and on the First Amendment right to protection of the communication of ideas:

> It is clear from the evidence in this case that psychotropic medication has the potential to affect and change a patient's mood, attitude and capacity to think. Whatever powers the constitution has granted our government, involuntary mind control is not one of them, absent extraordinary circumstances.[16]

The court found the defendants not liable for negligence because procurement of the necessary resources was not within their control: "It would be unjust and unreasonable to hold psychiatrists personally and individually responsible for resource deficiencies that are actually the 'responsibility of society.' "[17] In regard to the informed consent of patients taking medication, the court stated that treatment given despite lack of this consent was not considered below the medical standard of care in the period 1973 to 1975.

The *Rogers* decision was appealed to the First Circuit Court of Appeals, which rendered its findings in November 1980. The district court and the court of appeals agreed that patients have a right to refuse antipsychotic medications.[18] The court of appeals based its ruling on the due process clause of the Fourteenth Amendment "as security."[19] Since the court of appeals believed that the constitutional right to privacy was a sufficient basis for the right to refuse treatment, the court found it unnecessary to decide whether the district court was correct in finding that "the First Amendment rights of the plaintiffs were abridged by forcibly treating them with antipsychotic drugs."[20]

The appeals court ruled that dangerous patients could be medicated against their will. However, it found that the phrase "substantial likelihood of serious harm" lacked flexibility in implementation. The court concluded that the treating professionals must weigh the patient's interests against the need to prevent violence, balance the risk of harm against the beneficial effect that the drugs might have on the patient, and explore reasonable alternatives to the administration of medication. The court of appeals ordered that, on remand, the district court should set up procedural mechanisms, including an independent monitoring system, to provide for overseeing the medicating of potentially violent patients against their will.

The court of appeals affirmed the district court's decision regarding adjudication of an incompetent patient by the court. This, of course, can be a lengthy process. Consequently, the court of appeals ruled that a guardian did not have to be appointed if a delay could result in significant deterioration of the patient's mental health.[21] The appeals court stated that treatment decisions should be based on what the individual himself would have desired if he were competent to make that decision, and it instructed the district court to develop procedures to ensure that the decision-makers applied this substituted judgment test.[22]

Voluntary patients do have the right to refuse treatment, but the court of appeals stated:

> The Statute does not guarantee voluntary patients the treatment of their choice. Instead it offers a treatment regimen that state doctors and staff determine is best, and if the patient thinks otherwise, he can leave. We can find nothing even arguably unconstitutional in such a statutory scheme.[23]

Richard Cole, in reviewing the implications of *Rogers*, points out that many state hospital patients are of the lower socioeconomic class, who have nowhere else to go for treatment, and that these individuals might be faced with submitting to an "unwanted treatment or no treatment at all."[24] State institutions are their only treatment option. It is important to point out that voluntary patients who do not accept treatment, and who cannot be released to the community because of their mental condition, should be considered for involuntary commitment.

The court of appeals decision in *Rogers v. Okin* was appealed to the U.S. Supreme Court, which handed down an opinion in June 1982. It essentially remanded the case back to the court of appeals for review, taking into consideration a Massachusetts Supreme Court decision, *In the Matter of Guardianship of Richard Roe, III*, decided five months after the court of appeals decision in *Rogers v. Okin*.[25]

The First Circuit Court of Appeals subsequently remanded the case back to the federal district court and ordered it to "rule that the substantive and procedural rights of involuntarily committed patients set out in the *Roe* decision" were protected under the Fourteenth Amendment.[26]

Jarvis v. Levine

Jarvis v. Levine was decided in 1988 by the Minnesota Supreme Court. Mr. Jarvis had been committed to a security hospital since 1977 following his conviction for manslaughter in the shooting death of his sister.[27] He had completed his sentence and was diagnosed variously as having schizophrenia and/or a paranoid state. Although he was delusional about his medication, he was "articulate and intelligent" and could care for himself. The hospital in which Mr. Jarvis was located had a treatment review panel (TRP) to review medication refusals by patients. When Mr. Jarvis refused to take medication, the action was reviewed by the TRP. The TRP rejected and disapproved the request of the physician to medicate Mr. Jarvis involuntarily. This decision was later appealed to the medical director, who had the power to override the decision. A hospital review board could review the decision to determine whether procedural requirements were met; however, the board could not assess the clinical decision, nor could it overrule the medical director. Several times the decision was reviewed by all three reviewing forums. On three occasions the TRP disapproved authorization to involuntarily administer medications, and the hospital review board concurred. Two of the three times, the medical director overruled the decision, thus allowing injections of neuroleptic medication. A suit was brought by Mr. Jarvis under 42 USC, Section 1983, which reads as follows:

> *Civil action for deprivation of rights.* Every person who, under color of any statute, ordinance, regulation, custom, or usage, of any State or Territory or the District of Columbia, subjects, or causes to be subjected, any citi-

zen of the United States or other person within the jurisdiction thereof to the deprivation of any rights, privileges, or immunities secured by the Constitution and laws, shall be liable to the party injured in an action at law, suit in equity, or other proper proceeding for redress.[27]

An increasing number of lawsuits are being brought under this statute.

The case was appealed to the Supreme Court of Minnesota, which stated, "The ultimate issue underlying this case is whether state medical personnel may forcibly administer neuroleptic medications in *non*-emergency situations to a committed patient who refuses consent without prior court approval."[28] The court pointed out the possibility of side effects by writing, "the likelihood of some potentially devastating side effects is both sufficiently significant and well established to support a finding of intrusiveness."[29] The court continued by stating that the decision about whether to accept or reject a proposed medical regimen is a personal choice and not a medical decision: "The doctor may recommend, but does not dictate the final decision."

The Supreme Court of Minnesota ruled that there is a right to privacy under the Constitution of Minnesota. The court emphasized that this holding is based on the Minnesota Constitution and not "any law or provision of the United States Constitution."[30] Even though there was a treatment review process already in place in the state of Minnesota, an additional requirement was mandated to be implemented; that is, judicial approval was necessary prior to involuntary administration of neuroleptics in nonemergency situations, based on the intrusive nature of the treatment and right of privacy as enunciated in the state's constitution.[31]

Legal Bases for Refusal of Psychotropic Medication

According to Winick, there are several premises on which lawsuits over the right to refuse psychotropic medication have been grounded.[32] A number of lower state and federal court decisions have been predicated on the foundation that it is a violation of First Amendment rights of freedom of speech to forcibly inflict intrusive mental health treatment. Psychotropic drugs cause sedation and other side effects with which all nurses are familiar. In *Scott v. Plante*, the Third Circuit Court of Appeals ruled that involuntary administration of drugs to Mr. Scott, hospitalized with a diagnosis of schizophrenia after being found not guilty by reason of insanity, did interfere with his rights under the First Amendment.[33]

Many state and federal courts have based the right to refuse medication on the issue of privacy. Nurses are familiar with *Roe v. Wade*, the U.S. Supreme Court decision concerning abortion which stated that a woman's decision to elect an abortion was based on privacy issues.[34] The effects of psychotropic drugs on a person's ability to make decisions interfere, it is argued, with bodily privacy. As discussed in Chapter 3, the state's police power can be used as a justification for involuntary administration of drugs to persons exhibiting violent behavior.[35] The *parens patriae* power, the authority of the state to take an interest in citizens unable to provide for themselves, has also been used to forcibly medicate clients; however, documentation of the person's incompetency must be in evidence, and state law must be followed if it is mandated that a guardian be appointed.

The least restrictive alternative has been used to justify giving lithium and an antidepressant to a patient rather than a more "intrusive" antipsychotic medication.[36] The least restrictive alternative in relation to medication administration has not been ruled on by the U.S. Supreme Court. Analysis of treatment interventions by mental health personnel should be thoughtful and justified. Some authorities have stated that to use restraints for short periods of time is less intrusive than the forcible administration of neuroleptic drugs. We are aware of situations in which mental health professionals used four- and five-point restraints for several days. Is this procedure less restrictive than psychotropic medications? As Winick has stated, "The lower federal courts have consistently recognized that the federal constitution protects procedural due process in order to retain a liberty interest."[37] The Supreme Court in *Youngberg* discussed deferring to the professional judgment of the caregivers, and other courts have approved informal administration mechanisms rather than require court approval for involuntary administration.[38] Other courts, however, have stated that the judiciary must be involved in the decision whether to involuntarily administer psychotropic medication.

Research on the Right to Refuse Medication

Miller and Appelbaum have reviewed the literature on the refusal of medications.[39] They come to the following conclusions: Although short-term refusal is not infrequent, continuing long-term refusal is uncommon. Symptomatology such as delusions and denial may cause the refusal. Appelbaum comments that refusing individuals are generally sicker than compliant patients. Side effects have not been noted to be a major issue in causing refusal. Initially, those who refuse medication do not experience a remission of symptoms; however, if treated they seem to do as well as other patients. Miller reports that judicial reviewers disallow refusal of treatments more than do clinicians; independent reviewers reject more refusals than do in-house reviewers.[40] Miller believes the reason for the judiciary's stance is that, once a patient is committed, judges are reluctant to allow them to refuse treatment. Miller also points out that, "Since between 75% and 97% of persistent refusers are ultimately coerced to accept medications, the major result of the review process is to delay that treatment for periods of days to months, at costs to clinicians' time and financial resources."[41] Additional costs have been incurred in many states.

Aftermath of the Decisions

Two authors involved with the Massachusetts mental health system have reported the distress of staff members working in an environment under a restraining order. Michael J. Gill states that hostility, suspicion, and an adversarial quality entered relationships between patients and staff.[42] Although the federal court's opinion states that only 12 of 1,000 patients refused their medications between May 1, 1975, and June 23, 1977, both Gill and Schultz dispute this conclusion, citing higher figures.[43] They also note that the need to seclude patients increased.

In a report on 39 hearings for medication refusal in the state of Massachusetts in 1983–1984, 12 psychiatrists were engaged in the process, which consumed 411 hours. The physicians found the experience to be "painful," especially the experience of cross-examination.[44]

In New Jersey, Alexander Brooks comments, "Despite original resistance, apprehension and short–term problems that required straightening out, psychiatrists and other hospital staff have adjusted well to the modest requirements of *Rennie*."[45] Irwin Perr, however, writes that two patients hospitalized in private facilities in New Jersey incurred extra expenses of more than $30,000 because of the delay in treatment caused by their refusal to take medication, thus necessitating that an independent psychiatrist be brought in by the hospital.[46] Public advocates and attorneys were also brought in, adding to the expense.

Nursing Implications. Nurses are on the front line in the administration of medications. It is clear that voluntary patients do have the right to refuse medications and should not be forcibly medicated except in exceptional situations when the patient is actively violent to self and others and all less restrictive means have been unsuccessful. The behavior of the patient should be clearly described, with all prior therapeutic interventions recorded. Nurses must know and understand the guidelines laid down by the courts in the state where they practice in order to administer medication properly to involuntary patients. Although controversy remains about some legal decisions, there are elements of good clinical practice that can be adopted and encouraged by nurses now.

Scott Nelson writes that questions were generated about the administration of medication to patients not only because of basic constitutional questions but also as a result of concern about the adequacy of care and treatment and its documentation in patients' records within state hospitals. He proposes several guidelines to help ameliorate the situation: A recruitment plan should be developed to select professional personnel who meet the quality standards of practice. There should be some form of quality assurance and peer review of practices and procedures. Continuing education programs about psychotropic medications should be provided for hospital staff. A system should be developed to enable patients to participate actively in treatment decisions. There should be "meaningful patient advocacy."[47]

Beck describes the clinical assessment criteria to evaluate the competency of a mentally disabled person as follows: "A mentally disabled person is competent to refuse to take antipsychotic medication if he or she is aware of having a mental disorder; has sufficient knowledge about medication and mental disorder; and does not base the refusal on delusional beliefs."[48]

Sovner has developed guidelines for administration of medications as follows:

1. Has the patient been given a psychiatric diagnosis?

2. Is treatment consistent with the diagnosis?

3. Is there a set of clearly defined "target symptoms"?

4. Has the patient been informed about treatment outcome and side-effects?

5. Has a medical assessment been carried out prior to initiating drug therapy?

6. Are the therapeutic effects of treatment being regularly monitored?

7. Is the patient being regularly monitored for side-effects?

8. Is the patient receiving too many psychotropic agents?

9. Is the patient being undermedicated?

10. Is the patient being overmedicated?

11. Is drug therapy being changed too rapidly?

12. Are PRNs and stat doses being used excessively?

13. If the patient is being treated with an antipsychotic agent, are regular evaluations for tardive dyskinesia being conducted?

14. Is drug therapy being prescribed for an indefinite period of time?[49]

Scrak and Greenstein outline a procedure to be used when a client develops tardive dyskinesia. The procedure includes assessment of stability of symptoms for three months, and reduction of dose or discontinuance of medicine or selection of a different medication if symptoms persist. They point to an informal teaching program with clients and a collaborating working relationship among clients, nurses, and psychiatrists as helpful.[50]

Although this chapter has focused on three major cases, it should be emphasized that a state system or facility has the option to develop its own regulations for administering psychotropic medication if not under a court order. Nurses, of course, would want to have input in the development of these guidelines. Implementation of rules and regulations regarding the administration of medication would, it is hoped, prevent the abuse that leads to the filing of lawsuits.

Thomas Gutheil and Mark J. Mills remind caregivers in psychiatric settings that a reassuring therapeutic relationship is important in working with a drug-refusing patient: "A positive, caring relationship between staff and patient can play a vital role in reversing a treatment refusal."[51] A refusing patient should be asked daily if he wants to continue to turn down the medication. Nurses should not wait for litigation to be filed to become concerned about the issue. The controversy is here, and it is better to spend time writing well-conceived guidelines and implementing them than to plan a defense for a lawsuit.

Electroconvulsive Therapy

Electroconvulsive therapy (ECT) continues to be used throughout the United States. Joseph Morrissey and associates write that the administration of this treatment modality persists as one of the most "heated controversies in psychiatry."[52] Recent data, however, indicate that the use of ECT has diminished substantially in the law few years.[53]

In a study conducted in New York State, Morrissey found that the majority of ECT treatments were administered in private hospitals to middle-aged white women who had depressive components to their illness. In 1977, only 8% of persons receiving ECT were hospitalized in state mental hospitals.

The study concluded that, although there were probably some cases of contraindicated use of ECT, there was no widespread "pattern of misuse."[54] A more recent study indicates that, in 1980, 2.4% of all hospitalized patients in psychiatric facilities received ECT. Between the years 1975 and 1980, the utilization of ECT declined by 46%.[55]

A 1980 issue of *Nursing Law and Ethics* contains a nursing student's letter to the journal describing a situation that had been observed. A patient had revoked consent to ECT en route to the procedure. The patient was nevertheless held against her will, and the ECT was administered. The student's question was whether the procedure had been carried out in a legal manner. The response indicated that patients have a right to revoke consent unless they have been adjudicated incompetent and a guardian appointed.[56]

Competent voluntary patients clearly can refuse to submit to ECT.[57] Ennis and Emery point out that most states allow for substituted judgment regarding ECT.[58] A report published by the American Psychiatric Association states that if an incompetent patient's relatives are consulted and consent is given, this should be sufficient. "Good faith on the part of the patient's relatives and psychiatrist should be sufficient to ensure that what is being done, and done expeditiously, is in the best interests of the patient."[59] Parry advises that if the competency of an individual is in question, legal assistance should be sought or the courts petitioned for an adjudication.[60]

George Annas writes, "It is a general custom in the medical community to ask for the consent of the next of kin, and some judicial decisions imply that there is some authority vested in the next of kin."[61] He also comments that the only person who can legally make a binding decision for an incompetent person is a guardian. Therefore, it is imperative that state and case law be consulted and reviewed before allowing substituted judgment by a relative prior to administering ECT.

In an interesting case in California, the court of appeals affirmed a lower court decision that the city of Berkeley could not prohibit ECT from being administered within its boundaries. In 1982, the voters of Berkeley had adopted such an initiative, which was subsequently enacted into an ordinance. The suit was brought by the National Association of Private Psychiatric Hospitals and other psychiatric associations plus a psychiatrist and taxpayer to prevent the enforcement of the ordinance.[62]

Nursing Implications. Competent voluntary patients have the right to refuse ECT. In fact, some states have statutorily developed guidelines that define this right. However, there should be a policy and procedure within each facility outlining the mechanism to be used when a physician recommends that ECT be given to an incompetent voluntary or involuntary patient. Legal counsel for the facility should help in developing policies and procedures for implementation of the procedure so that they conform to statutes, case law, and rules and regulations that have been promulgated. Patients are entitled to receive adequate information upon which to base a decision regarding ECT, and they also have the right to alter their decision about the procedure up until the time it is administered. All principles of informed consent are applicable when obtaining consent for the procedure.

Psychosurgery

"Psychosurgery is defined as a destruction of some region of the brain in order to alleviate severe and otherwise intractable psychiatric disorders."[63] The treatment of physical symptoms resulting from strokes, tumors, or other pathologic disorders is not considered psychosurgery.[64] According to Robert Grimm, the number of psychosurgical procedures has decreased during the 1970s.[65]

Several states have passed statutes regulating the practice of psychosurgery. Since the passage of such legislation in Oregon and California, the practice of psychosurgery has been very limited in these states. A leading psychosurgery case, *Kaimowitz v. Department of Mental Health*, decided by a circuit court in Michigan and not officially reported, generated a great deal of publicity when the decision was rendered. The individual involved had been charged with murder and rape, was labeled a sexual psychopath, and had resided in an institution for 17 years. He was to undergo experimental brain surgery to determine if his behavior could be altered.[66] The court ruled that involuntarily detained individuals could not freely give truly informed consent. If the suggested procedure had been a routine surgical operation rather than an experimental psychosurgical procedure, the outcome might have been different.[67]

Annas advocates allowing competent patients who have been given adequate information and who can give informed consent to agree to psychosurgery, but he favors prohibiting the procedure for all patients who are incapable of making this decision because of mental incompetence.[68] His response to critics who suggest that this would eliminate an alternative for some patients is that it is a risk "well worth running, since the benefit is speculative but the harm produced by involuntary major surgery is not."[69]

Nursing Implications. Psychosurgery is not frequently performed. In facilities where the procedure is performed, policies and procedures for obtaining informed consent should be written and carried out based on statutory and case law and on any rules and regulations that have been promulgated.

References

1. *Rennie v. Klein*, 462 F.Supp. 1131 (N.J. 1978), at 1135.
2. Ibid., at 1136.
3. Carol R. Hartman: Pharmacotherapy. In Ann W. Burgess (ed.): *Psychiatric Nursing in the Hospital and the Community*, 3rd ed., Englewood Cliffs, N.J., 1981, p. 372.
4. Bernice Scrak and Robert Greenstein: Tardive Dyskinesia. *Journal of Psychosocial Nursing and Mental Health Services*, 125, no. 9, September 1987, pp. 24–27.
5. Dilop Jeste and Richard J. Wyatt: Tardive Dyskinesia: The Syndrome. *Psychiatric Annals*, 10, no. 1, January 1980, p. 16.
6. *Rennie v. Klein*, at 1153.
7. *Rennie v. Klein*, 476 F.Supp. 1294 (D. N.J. 1979), at 1298.
8. Ibid., at 1301.
9. Ibid.
10. Ibid., at 1312.
11. *Youngberg v. Romeo*, 457 U.S. 307 (1982), at 323.
12. Bruce Winick: The Right to Refuse Psychotropic Medication: Current State of the Law and Beyond. In David Rapoport and John Parry (eds.): *The Right to Refuse Antipsychotic Medication*, Washington, D.C., The American Bar Association's Commission of the Mentally Disabled, 1986, pp. 7–31.
13. *Rogers v. Okin*, 478 F.Supp. 1342 (D. Mass. 1979).
14. Ibid., at 1371.
15. Ibid.
16. Ibid., at 1366–1367.
17. Ibid., at 1385.
18. *Rogers v. Okin*, 634 F.2d 650 (1st Cir. 1980).
19. Ibid., at 653.
20. Richard Cole: The Patient's Right to Refuse Anti-Psychotic Drugs: The Court of Appeals Decision in *Rogers v. Okin*. *Medicolegal News*, 9, no. 1, February 1981, pp. 10–13, at 11.
21. *Rogers v. Okin*, 634 F.2d 650, (1st Cir. 1980), ftn. 16, at 660.
22. Ibid., at 661.
23. Ibid.
24. Cole: *The Patient's Right*, p. 14.
25. *In the Matter of Guardianship of Richard Roe, III*, 421 N.E.2d 40 (Mass. 1982).

26. Robert Miller: *Involuntary Civil Commitment of the Mentally Ill in the Post-Reform Era*, Springfield, Ill., Charles C Thomas, 1987, p. 142.
27. *Jarvis v. Levine*, 418 N.W.2d 139 (Minn. 1988).
28. Ibid., at 144.
29. Ibid., at 146.
30. Ibid., at 148.
31. Ibid.
32. Winick: The Right to Refuse Psychotropic Medication, pp. 8–26.
33. *Scott v. Plante*, 532 F.2d 939 (3rd Cir. 1976); vacated and remanded 458 U.S. 1101 (1982).
34. *Roe v. Wade*, 410 U.S. 113 (1978).
35. Winick: The Right to Refuse Psychotropic Medication, pp. 17–18.
36. Ibid., p. 18.
37. Ibid., p. 22.
38. *Youngberg v. Romeo*.
39. Miller: *Involuntary Civil Commitment*, pp. 150–156. Paul Appelbaum: Empirical Research on the Effects of Legal Policy on the Right to Refuse Treatment. In David Rapoport and John Parry (eds.): *The Right to Refuse Antipsychotic Medication*, Washington, D.C., The American Bar Association's Commission on the Mentally Disabled, 1986, pp. 87–100 (includes bibliographies of the reviewed research).
40. Miller: *Involuntary Civil Commitment*, p. 158.
41. Ibid.
42. Michael J. Gill: Side Effects of a Right to Refuse Treatment Lawsuit: The Boston State Hospital Experience. In Edward Doudera and Judith Swazey (eds.): *Refusing Treatment in Mental Health Institutions—Values in Conflict*, Ann Arbor, Mich., Association of University Programs in Health Administration Press, 1982, p. 82.
43. *Rogers v. Okin*, 478 F.Supp. 1342 (D. Mass. 1979), at 1369. Stephen Schultz: The Boston State Hospital Case: A Conflict of Civil Liberties and True Liberalism. *American Journal of Psychiatry*, 139, no. 2, February 1982, pp. 183–188.
44. Jorge Veliz and William James: Medicine Court: Rogers in Practice. *American Journal of Psychiatry*, 144, no. 1, January 1987, pp. 62–67 at 64.

45. Alexander D. Brooks: The Constitutional Right to Refuse Anti-Psychotic Medications. *Bulletin of the American Academy of Psychiatry and Law*, 8, no. 2, 179–221, 1980, at 213.
46. Irwin Perr: Effect of the Rennie Decision on Private Hospitalization in New Jersey: Two Case Reports. *American Journal of Psychiatry*, 138, no. 6, June 1981, pp. 774–778.
47. Scott Nelson: Should There Be a Right to Refuse Treatment? In Edward Doudera and Judith Swazey (eds.): *Refusing Treatment in Mental Health Institutions—Values in Conflict*, Ann Arbor, Mich., Association of University Programs in Health Administration Press, 1982, pp. 92, 93.
48. James C. Beck: Right to Refuse Antipsychotic Medication: Psychiatric Assessment and Legal Decision-Making. *Mental and Physical Disability Law Reporter*, 11, no. 5, September-October 1987, pp. 368–373 at 369.
49. Robert Sovner: Assessing the Quality of a Psychotropic Drug Regimen. In David Rapoport and John Parry (eds.): *The Right to Refuse Antipsychotic Medication*, Washington, D.C., The American Bar Association's Commission of the Mentally Disabled, 1986, pp. 48–57, at 55.
50. Scrak and Greenstein: Tardive Dyskinesia, pp. 24–26.
51. Thomas Gutheil and Mark J. Mills: Clinical Approaches with Patients Who Refuse Medication. In Edward Doudera and Judith Swazey (eds.): *Refusing Treatment in Mental Health Institutions—Values in Conflict*, Ann Arbor, Mich., Association of University Programs in Health Administration Press, 1982, p. 98.
52. Joseph Morrisey, Henry Steadman and Nancy Burton: A Profile of ECT Recipients in New York State During 1972 and 1977. *American Journal of Psychiatry*, 138, no. 5, May 1981, pp. 618–622, at 618.
53. Ibid., at 621, 622.
54. Ibid., at 622.
55. James Thompson and Jack Blaine: Use of ECT in the United States in 1975 and 1980. *American Journal of Psychiatry*, 144, no. 5, May 1987, pp. 557–562.
56. Mary Annas: Dear Mary. *Nursing Law and Ethics*, 1, no. 2, February 1980, p. 5.

57. American Psychiatric Association: *Electroconvulsive Therapy: Task Force Report 14*, Washington, D.C., American Psychiatric Association, 1978, p. 143.
58. Bruce Ennis and Richard D. Emery: *The Rights of Mental Patients (The Revised ACLU Guide to a Mental Patient's Rights)*, New York, Avon Books, 1978, p. 139.
59. American Psychiatric Association: *Electroconvulsive Therapy*, p. 143.
60. John Parry: Legal Parameters of Informed Consent Applied to Electroconvulsive Therapy. *Mental and Physical Disability Law Reporter*, 9, no. 3, May-June 1985, pp. 162–169.
61. George J. Annas, Leonard H. Glantz and Barbara F. Katz: *The Rights of Doctors, Nurses and Allied Health Professionals*, New York, Avon Books, 1981, p. 79.
62. *Northern California Psychiatric Society v. City of Berkeley*, 223 Cal. Rptr. 608 (1986).
63. Elliot Valenstein: Historical Perspective. In Elliot Valenstein (ed.): *The Psychosurgery Debate*, San Francisco, W. H. Freeman and Co., 1980, p. 12.
64. Ibid.
65. Robert J. Grimm: Regulation of Psychosurgery. In Elliot Valenstein (ed.): *The Psychosurgery Debate*, San Francisco, W. H. Freeman and Co., 1980, p. 437.
66. Francis C. Pizzulli: Psychosurgery Legislation and Case Law. In Elliot Valenstein (ed.): *The Psychosurgery Debate*, San Francisco, W. H. Freeman and Co., 1980, p. 382.
67. Samuel I. Shuman: The Concept of Informed Consent. In Elliot Valenstein (ed.): *The Psychosurgery Debate*, San Francisco, W. H. Freeman and Co., 1980, p. 442.
68. George J. Annas: Effective Psychosurgery: The Greater Danger? In Elliot Valenstein (ed.): *The Psychosurgery Debate*, San Francisco, W. H. Freeman and Co., 1980, p. 503.
69. Ibid.

CHAPTER 6

Forensic Issues

Forensic mental health services can be defined as those mental health services that are provided to persons who are also part of the criminal justice system; specifically, they are those services delivered to persons charged with or convicted of crimes or found to be guilty by reason of insanity. Traditionally, forensic services have been limited to (1) inpatient evaluation of pretrial defendants to assess their competency to stand trial and insanity at the time of the crime; (2) inpatient treatment of persons determined by the court to be either incompetent to stand trial or not guilty by reason of insanity; and (3) evaluation and treatment of persons convicted of crimes and placed in correctional facilities. However, as a result of court decisions in the 1970s, these services were expanded in a number of states to include the option of outpatient evaluation and treatment. Overall, the procedural changes required by the courts in forensic mental health services appear more dramatic than in any other area of mental health. However, because of the history of abuses in the forensic area, the long-term impact has been more limited.

Media exposés have kept the public informed about the abuses and problems that have occurred in both the judicial commitment of mental patients and the routine criminal justice process. As a result of this exposure, substantial changes have been made in criminal procedures and in judicial commitment procedures. However, few people are acquainted with the double stigma that attaches to persons who are labeled as being both mentally ill and a criminal. Imperfect as the procedures for commitment of the mentally ill or the resolution of criminal charges may have been, even these procedural protections usually were denied to those accused or convicted of a crime who were also determined to be mentally ill.

The primary explanation for the different set of procedures used for forensic patients was the theory that these patients posed a special danger to the public, and this distinction was the justification for the treatment provided to them. Unfortunately, the denial of due process to forensic patients frequently resulted in the lifelong detention of persons who were neither mentally ill nor convicted of a crime, or the detention of persons who, even if mentally ill or guilty of a crime, were held far beyond the maximum sentence they could have received had they actually been found guilty of the crime of which they were accused. Additionally, the privileges and services available to persons detained in "asylums for the criminally insane" were generally far inferior to those available in prisons.

Although in the 1970s the U.S. Supreme Court drastically limited the right of states to use a different set of procedures for certain forensic patients, many proposals for change continued the use of a separate set of procedures for this class of persons. Therefore, in analyzing issues related to forensic services, it is important to remember that no procedure should deny a forensic patient the same rights permitted to anyone else in the criminal justice system. He or she should also be provided appropriate mental health evaluation and necessary treatment in accordance with mental health statutes.

Forensic Evaluations

General Guidelines

There is a major distinction between a mental health professional providing direct service to a client and one providing forensic evaluation services. In performing forensic evaluations, the professional is normally providing not a direct service to a client but a service to a third party, such as a court. Because of this third-party relationship, it is imperative that the professional clearly inform the criminal defendant of the purpose of the evaluation and to whom the results will be reported.[1] The concepts of confidentiality and privilege cannot be applied in the same manner to information received from or about a forensic patient. In fact, the basis for the evaluation is usually a court order requiring the evaluation to take place. Obviously, if a professional has been retained by a defendant to provide services and to testify on his behalf, the guidelines will depend on the agreement between the parties.

Competency to Stand Trial

Competency to stand trial is a legal issue, not a clinical or medical one. The concept is based on the Fifth and Sixth Amendments to the U.S. Constitution. The Fifth Amendment protects an individual from deprivation of liberty without due process of law; the Sixth Amendment specifies the rights of an individual in a criminal prosecution, including the right to be informed about the nature and consequences of the accusation. If a person's mental condition prevents him from understanding the charges against him or from participating in his own defense, then he is incompetent to stand trial.

The specific criteria to be used by courts in determining competency to stand trial include an understanding of the nature of the legal process; a recognition of the consequences that could result from the accusation; and the ability to assist counsel in defense against the accusation. The U.S. Supreme Court in *Dusky v. United States*[2] clearly delineated these criteria. Although the most frequent reason for raising the question of competency is mental illness, other possibilities include mental retardation, physical impairment (such as deafness), and physical illness. Since the defendant must be competent in order to receive a fair trial, the judge and the prosecutor, as well as the defense attorney, have a duty to raise questions about the possible incompetency of a defendant. Once the issue is raised and the judge determines that there is sufficient cause to question a defendant's competency, the judge must order an evaluation by an appropriate professional and make a finding after the results of the evaluation have been received.

Until recently, only psychiatrists were considered qualified to conduct competency evaluations. Since there are only a limited number of psychiatrists available in the state systems, this requirement often resulted in prolonged inpatient evaluation in a large, centralized facility. However, in conjunction with other changes, many states now recognize that other professionals such as psychologists, social workers, and psychiatric nurses can perform these evaluations. Where such professionals are recognized, outpatient evaluations or speedy inpatient evaluations are most likely to be available to the courts.

One of the first comprehensive studies regarding the process of determining competency to stand trial was reported in a 1973 National Institute of Mental Health monograph entitled *Competency to Stand Trial and Mental Illness.* The principal investigator in the five-year study was Louis McGarry. Because irrelevant medical criteria had been applied by the psychiatric profession to the issue of competency, this study was designed to develop, validate, and demonstrate quantifiable clinical criteria to assess competency. For example, many psychiatrists would report to the court that a defendant was "psychotic" or "schizophrenic," or would use other psychiatric labels that did not assist the court in determining competency. This study also demonstrated that the courts themselves often confused the criteria for competency with the separate and different legal criteria for criminal responsibility. The result of the misunderstanding surrounding this issue was prolonged inpatient evaluation, even for defendants who were ultimately found to be competent.

The study demonstrated that evaluation for competency could be successfully performed on an outpatient basis by a variety of mental health professionals. If such screening determined the need for further evaluations, then an intensive and prolonged inpatient evaluation could be ordered. As a result, McGarry and his staff designed the Competency Assessment Instrument to help mental health professionals make evaluations by listing the pertinent legal issues involved. In addition to being tested in Massachusetts, this instrument has been used extensively in Tennessee, North Carolina, and Ohio.

There are other advantages to the use of outpatient evaluations for pretrial determinations of competency to stand trial. Frequently, a defendant's condition does not warrant hospitalization in order to make the competency decision, particularly if the professional performing the evaluation can adequately separate the clinical issues from the legal issue of competency. Therefore, when inpatient hospitalization is required for all evaluations, an increased amount of time is required to complete the evaluation, and the evaluation can delay trial. Also, when no outpatient services are available, there are limited support services for a defendant who is returned to jail. Finally, inpatient hospitalization, even if only for evaluation, tends to label a defendant as mentally ill or criminally insane and may make it more difficult to refute the criminal charges.

Criminal Responsibility (Insanity Defense)

Whereas competency to stand trial relates to the mental condition of the defendant at the time of evaluation, the issue of criminal responsibility, or the defense of not guilty by reason of insanity (NGRI), relates back to the mental condition of the defendant at the time of the crime of which he is accused. The legal standard is different and varies from state to state. A defendant must be competent to stand trial before he can utilize the defense of NGRI.

The evaluation for criminal responsibility is frequently ordered at the same time as the one for competency to stand trial. The evaluation can be conducted in a similar manner and by the same mental health professionals. However, some states, such as Tennessee, permit only psychiatrists or licensed clinical psychologists to perform criminal responsibility evaluations, although a variety of master's-level mental health professionals are recognized as able to perform competency evaluations.

The insanity defense has long been a part of the common law, the English law from which United States law evolved. The doctrine of *mens rea* first entered the English legal system more than eight centuries ago.[3] This doctrine states that the ability to form criminal intent is an inherent element of any offense. The intent to commit a crime is a critical element in proving a person guilty; the insanity defense is thus based on the theory that if a person's mental condition prevents him from forming the intent to commit a crime, he cannot be found guilty of the crime.

The insanity defense per se was first recognized by the courts in England in an 1843 murder case involving Daniel M'Naghten.[4] The standard known as the M'Naghten rule, which evolved from this case, relieves a person from responsibility for his acts if he was laboring under such a defect of reason—from a disease of the mind—as not to know the nature and quality of the act he was doing, or if he did know it, that he did not know that what he was doing was wrong.

The insanity defense has evolved in the law of all states, and for many years most states used a modified version of the M'Naghten rule. Criticism developed in the 1960s and 1970s about the outdated wording of the rule. A number of states then adopted the standard proposed by the American Law Institute. This rule states that a person is not responsible for criminal conduct if at the time of such conduct, as a result of mental disease or defect, he lacks substantial capacity either to appreciate the wrongfulness of his conduct or to conform his conduct to the requirements of the law. The terms *mental illness* and *defect* do not include an abnormality that is manifested only by repeated criminal or otherwise antisocial conduct.[5] Ironically, as discussed later in this chapter, the pendulum of change has swung in the other direction in the 1980s as the result of publicity about certain cases, and several states have changed back to the M'Naghten rule or some other more conservative test.[6]

Mental Health Services to Persons Convicted of Crimes

A defendant convicted of a crime is usually placed in a correctional facility. Since not all mentally ill defendants can utilize an insanity defense, an inmate may be mentally ill at the time of his conviction, or he may develop mental illness during incarceration. Although mental health services for inmates are frequently inadequate, most states have some services available. Some states refer all mental health problems to a central facility operated by the Department of Corrections or the Department of Mental Health. Others provide mental health services within the facility and utilize a unit within the institution when an inmate's condition requires segregation. Some authorities believe it is harmful to isolate mentally ill inmates from the general prison population. Such authorities also observe that the large facilities used for segregation have been greatly abused, with disruptive, aggressive, but nonpsychotic inmates becoming administratively defined as mentally ill.[7]

Until a 1965 U.S. Supreme Court decision, once an inmate was labeled mentally ill, particularly if he had been transferred to a segregated treatment facility, it was accepted practice for him to be denied parole hearings or even to be held beyond the expiration of his sentence. However, in *Baxstrom v. Herold*, the Supreme Court struck down this practice and asserted that a mentally ill prisoner cannot be held beyond the expiration of his term unless he is civilly committed to a mental health facility.[8] Additionally, the court later held, in *Vitek v. Jones*,[9] that an inmate cannot be transferred to a mental health facility against his will without a hearing. This issue is discussed in more detail in the next section.

Some states, such as California, statutorily provide for commitment directly to a facility other than a correctional institution immediately after conviction.[10] Other states label groups convicted of certain crimes, such as sex offenders, and maintain certain evaluation requirements for them, but do not otherwise refer them to the Department of Mental Health unless they are also clinically evaluated to be mentally ill.[11] However, special services may be provided within the Department of Corrections based on the nature of the crime. The philosophy of establishing separate categories, such as sexual offenders, and treating them differently because of the nature of the crime was developed in the 1950s. Since that time, however, the process of evaluation, treatment, and detention of the mentally ill has changed dramatically.

Many professionals now question whether the commitment of a convicted defendant to a mental health facility based on a label related to the criminal conviction (e.g., sex offender or drug abuser) rather than the person's mental condition can fulfill either a mental health goal or a correctional goal.[12] In states where such commitment is authorized, if a prisoner is in fact not mentally ill, he may still be hospitalized because of the type of crime he committed. Even if the person committed to the mental health facility is actually mentally ill, the correctional goal and the mental health goal may be entwined in such a manner as to be confusing to the public, to the person so committed, and to the treating facility. This is particularly true when the person is given an "indefinite" *sentence* to a treatment facility, with release based on response to "treatment." Some experts have concluded that the best approach would be to abolish the quasi-criminal status, classify all persons convicted and sentenced as prisoners, and provide services to those who are mentally ill.[13.]

However, in *Allen v. Illinois* the U.S. Supreme Court in fact upheld the indefinite commitment statute in Illinois.[14] The issue the defendant raised in this case was whether he could utilize the privilege against self-incrimination when facing commitment under this statute. The court stated that this privilege was available only in criminal proceedings or in other circumstances "where the answers might incriminate [a defendant] in future criminal proceedings."[15] The court further stated that the defendant failed to demonstrate that the scheme was "so punitive either in purpose or effect as to negate [the state's] intention that it be civil."[16]

Justice Stevens dissented on behalf of four justices, stating, "When the criminal law casts so long a shadow on a putatively civil proceeding, I think it is clear that the procedure must be deemed a 'criminal case' within the meaning of the fifth amendment."[17] Stevens' dissent further states that if a proceeding to commit a sexually dangerous person may escape characterization as criminal simply because "a goal is treatment...nothing would prevent the State from creation of an entire corpus of 'dangerous person' statutes to shadow its criminal code," resulting in the "evisceration of criminal law and its accompanying protections."[18]

"Criminal" Commitments

Treatment of Forensic Patients

Once a person involved in the criminal justice system has been evaluated and found to be mentally ill and in need of treatment, the manner in which the person may be committed and treated depends on his legal category. As stated previously, it is only as a result of recent U.S. Supreme Court decisions that many forensic patients, such as pretrial incompetent defendants, are now provided the same due process protections as civil patients who are judicially committed. However, in some instances the commitment procedures used for forensic patients still vary from those for civil commitments, and therefore these procedures are discussed as separate categories.

Incompetent Defendants

The greatest changes produced by judicial decisions in forensics have occurred in the area of long-term commitment of pretrial defendants. Previously, a pretrial defendant found incompetent to stand trial would be committed indefinitely to a maximum-security facility solely on the basis of his incompetency. The commitment lasted until he became competent. Thus, defendants who had been found neither guilty of a crime nor mentally ill under civil commitment standards were frequently detained for longer periods than if they had actually been found guilty of the crime of which they were accused.[19]

In 1972, in *Jackson v. Indiana*, the U.S. Supreme Court ruled that a defendant could not be detained indefinitely in a mental hospital solely on the basis of his incompetency to stand trial.[20] Theon Jackson was a mentally retarded deaf mute with limited ability to communicate. He was found to be incompetent to stand trial on two counts of robbery involving a total of nine dollars; because his condition would not change, he would never become competent. At the time of the Supreme Court hearing, he had been detained three and one-half years. Since Indiana law required an incompetent defendant to be detained in a mental hospital until he became competent, Mr. Jackson had effectively received a life sentence.

The major impact of this decision was to mandate that the hospitalization of pretrial defendants be limited to a reasonable period of time for the purposes of assessing competency to stand trial and treating incompetents to help them become competent. However, the court held that if a defendant is not likely to become competent in the foreseeable future, he must be either committed according to the same standards used for civilly committed patients or released from detention. The Supreme Court did not define "reasonable period of time" but found that the three and one-half years Jackson had been held was too long.

Most states had statutes similar to Indiana's and were faced with the mandate to change. One state, Tennessee, decentralized its forensic services to provide outpatient evaluations for pretrial defendants whenever possible.[21] If inpatient evaluation or treatment is required, the court may order 30 days' hospitalization. However, after that period, a defendant must be civilly committed in order to be detained further in the hospital.[22] Other states have continued to use different commitment standards for periods less than three and one-half years, or they have related the length of commitment to the length of the sentence for the crime of which the defendant has been accused but not convicted.[23]

Some commentators have speculated that the *Jackson* decision has produced a dilemma for several states because of the number of defendants who are incompetent but do not meet civil commitment standards. Therefore, they can neither be detained in a mental hospital nor proceed to trial, and consequently must be released.[24] However, statistics from Tennessee, a state that has developed a comprehensive pretrial evaluation system that also provides support services in the jails, dispute this conclusion. In 1987, 1,212 defendants were evaluated on an outpatient basis; only 403 of these were referred for inpatient evaluation, and of these, only 41 were civilly committed because they were incompetent to stand trial.[25] An uncertain but small number of defendants were found to be incompetent but not committable.

Persons Found Not Guilty by Reason of Insanity

Procedures for placement of a defendant found NGRI vary from state to state. Until changes in mental health laws were made in the 1970s, these persons were automatically committed to a mental health facility without regard for their mental condition at the time of commitment. If the person was found to be no longer dangerous, release had to be ordered by the criminal court.[26]

There has been increased recognition that a person found NGRI may not be currently mentally ill or in need of hospitalization. Legally, a person found NGRI is not guilty of the crime; therefore, this person cannot be sent to prison to receive punishment. However, the procedure of automatic and indefinite detention in a hospital provides a similar alternative under the guise of providing treatment.

The legal system in many instances has recognized that continued hospitalization should be related to the person's current mental condition, not his mental condition at the time of the crime.[27] However, there has been disagreement among courts in various jurisdictions as to whether an NGRI patient can be treated differently from a civil patient. Some courts have held that such a patient can be held for a short period of evaluation regardless of mental condition, but for long-term hospitalization he must be civilly committed in the same manner as any other person.[28] Other courts have ruled that a different standard of commitment can be used.[29] The U.S. Supreme Court has now determined that it is not a denial of equal protection for a person found NGRI to be committed in a different manner from a civil patient.

In *Jones v. United States*,[30] the court upheld the constitutionality of the District of Columbia's automatic commitment statute for persons found not guilty by reason of insanity on the basis that an acquittal based on insanity established beyond a reasonable doubt the fact that the defendant committed a criminal act, and this fact provides "concrete evidence as to the person's dangerousness that is generally 'as persuasive as any predictions about dangerousness' made regularly in commitment proceedings."[31] The court further held that there was no reason to adopt the higher standard of proof of "clear and convincing evidence" that this same court required in *Addington v. Texas*,[32] and that a person is not eligible for release because he was hospitalized for a period longer than he could have been incarcerated if convicted. The court, in defending its decision, stated that its holding was in accordance with the widely and reasonably held view that insanity acquittees constitute a special class that should be treated differently from other candidates for commitment.[33]

In regard to the release of an NGRI from the hospital, some states still require court approval, whereas others permit the hospital to make the release decision. Unlike with the issue of commitment, most courts have agreed that it is constitutionally permissible to use a more stringent release standard for people who have been found NGRI than for other committed patients.[34] However, there is some disagreement regarding the standard to be used. Since John Hinckley's acquittal for shooting President Reagan in 1981, numerous states have revised their release standards, as demonstrated in a table in a recent article showing the various reforms that have occurred.[35]

Persons Convicted of Crimes. The final category of commitment concerns persons convicted of crimes and sent to prison. As discussed previously, an inmate may be transferred to a mental health facility during his imprisonment. However, he cannot be transferred against his will unless adequate due process procedures are provided. The court in *Vitek v. Jones* stated:

> Involuntary commitment to a mental hospital is not within the range of conditions of confinement to which a prison sentence subjects an individual. While a conviction and sentence extinguish an individual's right to

freedom from confinement for the term of his sentence, they do not authorize the State to classify him as mentally ill and to subject him to involuntary psychiatric treatment without affording him additional due process protections. Here, the stigmatizing consequences of a transfer to a mental hospital for involuntary psychiatric treatment, coupled with the subjection of the prisoner to mandatory behavior modification as a treatment for mental illness, constitute the kind of deprivations of liberty that require procedural protections.[36]

The only way a prisoner can be held beyond the expiration of his sentence because of mental illness is by civil commitment to a mental health facility.[37]

Emerging Issues

During the 1970s, new procedures were proposed in the forensic area and mandated by court decisions. In the 1980s the focus of proposed change has been primarily on the use of the insanity defense. Several experts have taken the position that the insanity defense is abused and that psychiatry should not be involved in the criminal justice system.[38] They have proposed that the insanity defense therefore be abolished. However, there is a serious legal question as to whether or not this would be unconstitutional.

The U.S. Supreme Court has not ruled on the issue of abolishing the insanity defense. However, at least two state courts have reviewed the issue. The dates of these court cases indicate that the idea of abolishing the insanity defense is not, in fact, new. The Washington legislature attempted to abolish the insanity defense in 1910, but the Supreme Court of Washington declared the legislative action to be unconstitutional and restored the use of the insanity defense.[39] Later in the century, in 1931, Mississippi also attempted to abolish the insanity defense; again, the State Supreme Court declared the action unconstitutional.[40] More recently, many other states have attempted to "reform" the insanity defense.[41]

As discussed earlier in this chapter, the insanity defense is a concept deeply rooted in our legal history, along with the requirement of *mens rea*, or intent, for a criminal act. U.S. Supreme Court decisions in other areas regarding the requirement of intent to prove criminal conduct imply that the court might not permit abolition of the insanity defense.[42] Also, the weight of scholarly opinion favors its retention.[43.]

Over the years there have been several other recommendations to limit but not abolish the insanity defense. One of these recommendations is the use of a bifurcated trial procedure for a defendant who relies on the insanity defense. California first adopted the procedure in 1927.[44] Under this procedure, there are two trials: The first determines whether a criminal act was committed and, if so, whether the accused committed the act. If the accused is found guilty, a second trial is held for the sole purpose of determining whether the accused was insane at the time he committed the criminal act.

This legislation was designed to separate the element of intent from the question of guilt, thereby delaying the issue of intent until the second trial. The attempt has not been entirely successful, however. The California courts have allowed evidence of diminished capacity, a legal defense related to the issue of intent, to be used during the first trial.[45] Although several states have tried this concept, as of February 1978 only California, Colorado, and Wisconsin retained the bifurcated system. All three states permit the issue of intent to be introduced at the first trial.[46]

The Supreme Courts of Arizona, Florida, and Wyoming have declared the bifurcated trial system unconstitutional.[47] The Florida Supreme Court stated:

The principal issue presented for our consideration is whether the bifurcated trial system established by statute for the adjudication of guilt and insanity in criminal trail denies a defendant his right to due process of law under the state and federal constitutions. We...hold...that procedure unconstitutional.[48]

Therefore, there are in fact no states that currently provide for a pure bifurcated trial procedure. Those states that began with such systems either modified them by legislative amendment or court decision to cure the constitutional imperfections, repealed the procedure, or declared it unconstitutional. The bifurcated system, at least as it was originally envisioned, has been destroyed. In order to correct the unconstitutional aspects of the procedure, it has been altered to admit the very evidence the system was originally designed to restrict.[49]

Perhaps as the result of the failure of these past efforts to limit the use of the insanity defense, legislation has now emerged to allow a new type of plea: "guilty but mentally ill" (GBMI). This concept was first adopted in Michigan; other states that have followed suit include Indiana, Illinois, and Georgia.[50.]

One of the reasons for the popular move to pass such "GBMI" legislation is the misperception that such legislation abolishes the insanity defense. In fact, the legislation leaves the plea of NGRI as it stands; the proposed plea of GBMI would be available to defendants who have already pleaded NGRI but were, in fact, found guilty. The original proponents speculated that the GBMI plea would provide a jury with an option, thereby reducing the number of successful insanity defenses. However, in Michigan the statistics show the opposite result.[51] In a six-month period in 1975, Michigan performed 92 insanity defense evaluations; in 15 of these the defendants were found insane. In a comparable six-month period in 1979, after implementation fo the GBMI legislation, 589 evaluations for the insanity defense were performed, and 50 defendants were found to be NGRI.

Because the GBMI classification introduces new issues related to mental illness and criminal responsibility, there has been an increase in the number of defendants requesting, and attempting to use in their defense, pretrial psychiatric evaluations. The most obvious contradiction inherent in the concept and application of the guilty but mentally ill plea is its reliance on *past* mental condition (at the time of the crime) for *present* treatment. If someone who pleads GBMI goes to prison, he receives treatment priority over a prisoner who developed mental illness in prison or did not plead GBMI. Otherwise, the legislation produces little change, since most states are required to provide mental health services to prisoners.

Perhaps the real intent behind this legislation can be identified in the provisions that place extra evaluation requirements on an individual pleading GBMI. For example, a GBMI inmate who is given probation must remain on probation no less than five years; a GBMI inmate cannot be released without psychiatric evaluation, even if he would otherwise be eligible for parole, before the sentence is up. It would appear that the reason for this legislation is the continued fear that there are large numbers of persons, both mentally ill and criminal, who are particularly dangerous and must receive special treatment. Recent studies have examined the specific results of the GBMI verdict and strongly suggest that many of the legislative intents of such insanity defense reforms are not met.[52]

Another issue that developed in the 1970s was the application of the right to treatment in a forensic setting. The case that extensively considered this issue was *Davis v. Watkins*.[53] The court reviewed the care provided at Lima State Hospital in Ohio and mandated that treatment programs be initiated.

One additional issue that has been raised relates to the provision of expert testimony and is reviewed in *Estelle v. Smith*.[54] This case involved a pretrial psychiatric evaluation to determine the competency of a defendant to stand trial on the charge of first-degree murder in which the state intended to seek the death penalty. After conviction, the same psychiatrist who had evaluated the defendant for competency testified on the issue of dangerousness to society at the sentencing hearing. Since the state used as evidence against the defendant the details of disclosures made during the pretrial psychiatric evaluation, the court held that it violated the defendant's Fifth Amendment privilege against self-incrimination. The case ruling implies that if a pretrial evaluation is limited to determination of competency and insanity and is not used as evidence against a defendant—other than in relation to the insanity defense—the defendant's constitutional right against self-incrimination has not been violated.

Two additional U.S. Supreme Court cases in the forensic area are *Barefoot v. Estelle*[55] and *Ake v. Oklahoma*.[56] In *Barefoot v. Estelle* the court upheld the use of psychiatric testimony regarding future dangerousness at the penalty phase of a case, even where the testimony is offered in response to a hypothetical question and the expert witness did not personally examine the defendant.[57] Two years later, in *Ake v. Oklahoma*, the court reviewed the issue of expert testimony in an entirely different context of the scope of a defendant's right to expert assistance in establishing an insanity defense. The court held that when an indigent "defendant has made a preliminary showing that his sanity at the time of the offense is likely to be a significant factor at trial, the Constitution requires that a state provide access to a psychiatrist's assistance on this issue if the defendant cannot otherwise afford one."[58]

Nursing Implications. The best policy for a nurse providing pretrial evaluation is to limit herself to an evaluation of the person's present condition or competency to stand trial. The nurse should attend educational programs to learn the use of the appropriate assessment tools. It is recommended that only nurses with master's-level degrees in psychiatric-mental health nursing testify on this issue. Also, an expert who reports an evaluation as a friend of the court is less likely to be viewed as an adversary of the defendant.

Conclusion

This chapter reviews the issues related to the provision of forensic services. The main goals in providing these services are to assist the courts with pretrial evaluations and to provide support services to mentally ill persons charged with or convicted of a crime so that their charges can be resolved fairly and in a manner similar to that used for other defendants. The evaluator's role is normally that of a friend of the court.

The criminal justice system has been forced to become more directly involved with more mentally ill defendants for a number of reasons. First, modern technology has permitted a large number of persons to be treated in the community rather than be institutionalized. Second, traditionally, pretrial defendants who were mentally ill were automatically detained in mental hospitals, and the courts were rarely confronted with final disposition of these defendants. Finally, if a defendant was found NGRI, automatic indefinite detention was the result. Now the courts are required to deal on an individual basis with these defendants.

The lawyers and judges involved in the criminal justice system frequently do not understand mental illness, however, and are hesitant to deal with the mentally ill defendant. Although court decisions now permit mentally ill defendants to proceed to trial and not be detained indefinitely without a proper hearing, new recommendations are being made that would once again permit the indefinite incarceration of mentally ill defendants. In reviewing the various cases of the 1980s and attempting to assess the position of the U.S. Supreme Court in this area, it is difficult to find a consistent approach. Some of the cases barely mask a repressive, punitive attitude in the name of "procedural defaults," whereas others present some doctrinal threads based on the court's "rockbottom focus on 'fundamental fairness' " or the "fundamental miscarriage of justice" rule.[59]

After consistently noting in earlier cases the vagaries and unreliability of psychiatric testimony in civil cases, the court upheld the admission of broad-ranging psychiatric evidence in *Barefoot*. Additionally, in *Jones* it upheld a statutory scheme that is almost unanimously unsupported by psychiatric knowledge.[60] However, in *Ake* the court again acknowledged the problems with psychiatric testimony by stating that an ambiguity of psychiatric knowledge risks an inaccurate resolution of sanity issues, thus compelling that expert testimony be provided to indigents.[61] Perhaps the court will one day adopt the philosophy of C. J. Schoenfield that the law can avoid imposing criminal liability upon the insane "because punishing them, unlike punishing criminals, fails to serve the public's inner needs."[62]

Any recommendation that proposes to treat the mentally ill defendant or prisoner in a manner that deviates from the regular procedures should be suspect.[63] History demonstrates extensive abuse when deviation from the use of regular procedures is permitted.[64]

We are still faced with the unpopularity of the mentally ill defendant within the criminal justice system and among the public at large. One hopes that rationality and basic legal principles will prevail in this atmosphere, particularly in the aftermath of the acquittal of John Hinckley for his attempt on the life of a U.S. president.

References

1. Jonas Rappeport: Forensic and General Psychiatry. *American Journal of Psychiatry*, 139, March 1982, pp. 331–334, at 332.
2. *Dusky v. United States*, 362 U.S. 402 (1960).
3. Paul S. Appelbaum: The Insanity Defense. *Law and Psychiatry*, 33, no. 1, January 1982, pp. 13–14.
4. Ibid.
5. *Graham v. State of Tennessee*, 547 S.W.2nd 531 (Tenn. 1977).
6. Lisa Callahan, Connie Mayer and Henry J. Steadman: Insanity Defense Reform in the United States—Post-Hinckley. *Mental and Physical Disability Law Reporter*, 11, no. 1, February 1987, pp. 54–59, at 57.
7. Loren H. Roth: Correctional Psychiatry. In William J. Curran (ed.): *Modern Legal Medicine, Psychiatry and Forensic Science*, Philadelphia, F. A. Davis Co., 1980, pp. 682, 687.
8. *Baxstrom v. Herold*, 383 U.S. 107 (1965).
9. *Vitek v. Jones*, 445 U.S. 480 (1980).
10. *California v. Ginese*, 175 Cal. Rptr. 383 (Cal. Ct. App. 1981).
11. *Tennessee Code Annotated*, 33-6-301 through 305.
12. Roth: Correctional Psychiatry, p. 679.
13. National Institute of Mental Health: *Mental Health and the Law: A System in Transition* (Crime and Delinquency Issues Monograph Series, DHEW Publication No. [ADM] 75–176), Washington, D.C., Government Printing Office, 1973, p. 192.
14. *Allen v. Illinois*, 478 U.S. 364 (1986).
15. Ibid., at 374.
16. Ibid., at 374.
17. Ibid., at 389.
18. Ibid., at 389; and Michael L. Perlin: The Supreme Court and the Mentally Disabled Criminal Defendant: Recent Developments. *Bulletin of the American Academy of Psychiatry and the Law*, 15, no. 4, 1987, pp. 391–409, at 397.
19. James S. Walach: The Incompetency Plea: Abuses and Reforms. *The Journal of Psychiatry and Law*, 8, no. 3, 1980, pp. 318–319. Joyce K. Laben and Lona D. Spencer: Decentralization of Forensic Services. *Community Mental Health Journal*, 12, no. 4, 1976, pp. 405–414.

20. *Jackson v. Indiana*, 406 U.S. 715 (1972).
21. *Tennessee Code Annotated*, 33-7-301(a). Joyce K. Laben, Mark Kashgarian, Donald B. Nessa and Lona D. Spencer: Reform From the Inside: Mental Health Center Evaluation of Competency to Stand Trial. *Journal of Community Psychology*, 5, 1977, pp. 52–62.
22. *Tennessee Code Annotated*, 33-7-301(b).
23. Ronald Roesch and Stephen C. Coldberg: Treatment and Disposition of Defendants Found Incompetent to Stand Trial: A Review and a Proposal. *International Journal of Law and Psychiatry*, 2, 1979, pp. 349–370.
24. Ralph Slovenko: The Developing Law on Competency to Stand Trial. *Journal of Psychiatry and Law*, 5, no. 2, Summer 1977, pp. 165–200.
25. Tennessee Department of Mental Health and Mental Retardation: Management Information System, Marthagem Whitlock, Director of Specialized Services.
26. Abraham S. Goldstein: *Insanity Defense*, New Haven, Conn., Yale, University Press, 1967.
27. *Powell v. Florida*, 579 F.2d 324 (5th Cir. 1978). See also *Bernham et al. v. Edwards et al.*, No-80-9052 (No. Dist. Ga., May 27, 1982).
28. *United States v. Cohen*, No-80-00382 (D.C. Cir., March 5, 1982).
29. *Pohley v. Psychiatric Security Review Board*, 632 P.2d 15 (Ore. Ct. App. 1981). See also *Colorado v. Chavez*, 629 P.2d 1040 (Colo. Sup. Ct. 1978).
30. *Jones v. United States*, 463 U.S. 354 (1983).
31. Ibid., at 363–364. Perlin: The Supreme Court and the Mentally Disabled Criminal Defendant, p. 392.
32. *Addington v. Texas*, 441 U.S. 418 (1979).
33. Ralph Reisner: *Law and the Mental Health System, Civil and Criminal Aspects*, Minneapolis, West Publishing Co., 1985.
34. *Illinois v. Valdez*, 447 U.S. 410 (1979).
35. Callahan, Mayer and Steadman: Insanity Defense Reform in the United States, p. 57.
36. *Vitek v. Jones*, 445 U.S. 480 (1980).
37. *Baxstrom v. Herold*, 383 U.S. 107 (1965).
38. Richard A. Pasework and Mark O. Pasework: Cuckoo's Nest. *Journal of Psychiatry and Law*, 6, Winter 1978, pp. 481–498.
39. *State v. Strasberg*, 60 Wash. 106 (1910), at 120.

40. *Sinclair v. State*, 161 Miss. 142, 132 So. 581 (1931).
41. Callahan, Mayer and Steadman, Insanity Defense Reform in the United States, p. 54.
42. *Palko v. Connecticut*, 302 U.S. 319 (1937). *Wolf v. Colorado*, 338 U.S. 25 (1949).
43. The Insanity Defense. Should It Be Abolished? *Newsweek*, May 24, 1982, p. 61.
44. *California Penal Code*, Section 1026.
45. *People v. Corshem*, 51 Col.2d 716, 337 P.2d 492 (1959). See also *People v. Wells*, 33 Cal.2d 330, 202 P.2d 53 (1949).
46. Susan Moseley: The Insanity Defense: An Old Procedure Under New Attack. Vanderbilt University School of Law, May 1979.
47. Ibid.
48. *State ex rel. Boyd v. Green*, 335 So.2d 789 (Fla. 1978), p. 790.
49. Moseley: The Insanity Defense, p. 18.
50. Michigan Code Annotated, Section 28, 1059.
51. Michael L. Cross and Robert D. Racine: *Impact of Change in Legal Standard for Those Adjudicated Not Guilty by Reason of Insanity*, Ann Arbor, Mich., Center for Forensic Psychiatry, 1980.
52. Callahan, Mayer and Steadman: Insanity Defense Reform in the United States, note 35, p. 59.
53. *Davis v. Watkins*, 384 F.Supp 1196 (N.D. Ohio 1974). See also *Davis v. Balson*, 461 F.Supp 842 (N.D. Ohio 1978).
54. *Estelle v. Smith*, 41 U.S. L.W. 4492 (1981).
55. *Barefoot v. Estelle*, 463 U.S. 880 (1983).
56. *Ake v. Oklahoma*, 470 U.S. 68 (1985).
57. *Barefoot v. Estelle*, at 896–899.
58. *Ake v. Oklahoma*, at 69.
59. Perlin: The Supreme Court and the Mentally Disabled Criminal Defendant, pp. 399–402.
60. Ibid.
61. Ibid.
62. C. J. Schoenfield: Psychoanalysis Applied to the Law, 31, 1984, discussing Schoenfield: Laws and Unconscious Mental Mechanisms. *Bulletin of the Menninger Clinic*, 28, no. 23, 1984, p. 28.
63. National Institute of Mental Health: *Mental Health and the Law*, p. 192.
64. Wendell R. Rais: *Cold Storage*. New York, Simon and Schuster, 1980.

CHAPTER 7

The Rights of Children

In most states, for most purposes, a juvenile or minor is defined as any individual less than 18 years old.[1] Minors are presumed incompetent to make most decisions themselves, and the parent is the legally appropriate person to provide legal consent for actions affecting a juvenile. For example, a minor is not legally competent to execute a will, sign a contract, or consent to medical treatment. Nor does he have the right to engage in certain activities, such as voting, even with the consent of the parent. Many states have now raised to above 18 the age at which the purchase of beer or liquor is permitted.[2]

There are, however, exceptions to the presumption of legal incompetence of a juvenile. Some states have statues that specify exceptions and permit juveniles to act in their own behalf in certain areas. Exceptions include the right to seek treatment for drug abuse, the right to consent to contraception, and the right to seek psychiatric treatment.[3] However, states vary in the number of and the age requirements for these exceptions.[4] Also, a legal exception for one issue does not extend to other issues related to the juvenile.[5] The exceptions are based on the "mature minor concept," which gives legal validity to the consent of older minors to treatment when they are capable of demonstrating the degree of intelligence and the maturity of judgment necessary to "satisfy the adult informed consent model."[6]

In addition to the statutory exceptions regarding the legal incompetence of juveniles, other factors may change the age at which a juvenile may act on his own behalf. Children can become emancipated from parental control through acts of independence such as marriage or enlistment in the armed forces, through failure of the parents to meet their legal responsibilities, or through judicial decree.[7]

Emancipation is the oldest concept that recognizes circumstances under which the child-parent relationship can be severed prior to the child obtaining the age of majority. A more recent application of this doctrine has been the recognition that modern society makes children grow up faster; this has resulted in legislation in some states to provide mature minors with some recourse for obtaining legal recognition as adults.[8] The doctrine of emancipation permits a minor to assume the rights and responsibilities of adulthood regardless of age.[9] Emancipation may occur as a result of a judicial decree or automatically as a result of a statute.

Historically, the common-law doctrine of emancipation developed primarily to benefit parents and to provide a way for them to relinquish, expressly or implicitly, control of minor children. When this control is relinquished, the minor is required to function as an adult, and the parent is relieved of any obligation to support the minor. On the other hand, emancipation may also occur when a parent deserts the minor or is guilty of nonsupport. Common-law emancipation is conditioned on an act or omission of the parent.[10] The exceptions are emancipation by marriage or service in the armed forces. However, normally the minor needs the parent's consent for either of these to occur.

Common-law emancipation did little to resolve conflicts between parent and child. Fourteen states now have laws that permit any minor seeking adult status to petition the court and, if he meets the criteria, to be granted adult status.[11] Although some of the statues enacted in past years were based on common–law emancipation, later ones were designed to promote the independence of minors who demonstrate maturity.

In addition, even if a juvenile is emancipated, his minority status may still be preserved for some purposes. For example, some states still require parental consent for general medical treatment even if a juvenile is married or emancipated.[12]

Until the litigation of the past two decades, the issues related to children centered on the ability of juveniles to consent or to act in their own behalf. However, legal activity concerning children has increasingly focused on efforts to "define, expand, and enforce their rights both in relation to families and in relation to broader social systems."[13] The result of this litigation has been to raise questions and change laws in new areas regarding the rights of juveniles.

Litigation concerning the rights of children in relation to their families can be divided into four areas: (1) when children should have access to independent legal representation; (2) when the grounds are appropriate for removing children from their families and terminating the rights of parents; (3) when parental decisions about children should be reviewed by the court; and (4) when juveniles should be permitted to make decisions independently of their parents.[14]

All four issues can potentially affect the services provided by mental health professionals. Professionals are involved not only in providing direct services to juveniles, but also in providing indirect services by participating in the evaluation of parents and in reporting to courts when custody or neglect are at issue. Issues (1) and (2) apply to these activities. Categories (3) and (4) more directly affect the day-to-day treatment provided by mental health professionals to minors, because they specify when a parent may consent to psychiatric treatment for a child, regardless of the child's wishes, and when a child may consent to his own psychiatric treatment, regardless of his parent's position.

One of the most controversial issues reviewed by the courts is the right of parents in most states to commit their children for treatment at inpatient psychiatric facilities voluntarily. In this situation, unlike an adult, the juvenile does not have a right to a court hearing if he objects to his hospitalization, nor in most states does he have the right to request his own release. In the 1970s, a number of lawsuits contesting this practice were filed. They argued that the practice was unconstitutional, and that a court hearing should always be held to determine whether or not a juvenile should be committed. Subsequently, some states amended their statues to provide more rights to juveniles in the process of admission to psychiatric hospitals. For example, Tennessee amended its statute to permit juveniles older than 16 to admit themselves to psychiatric hospitals voluntarily, and it authorized juveniles of all ages to request their own release.[15] The same changes also determined whether the parent of the child may consent to treatment options such as psychotropic medication and participation in research.

Whether a child is receiving outpatient or inpatient treatment, there is the additional issue of who can authorize release of medical information. If a state acknowledges the right of a "mature minor" to consent to psychiatric treatment, the child probably is the appropriate person to consent to release of information. If the child refuses to consent to release information at the same time that a parent is demanding its release, the mental health facility can be placed in a very awkward position, particularly if the parent is paying for the service. In cases where such a legal dilemma can arise, this issue should be clarified before treatment is started.

This issue was finally reviewed by the U.S. Supreme Court in *Parham v. J. L. & J. R.*[16] In this case, the court held that a formal court hearing is not required to determine whether a minor can be voluntarily admitted to a psychiatric facility. The court upheld the rights of parents to admit their children to mental hospitals if a neutral physician agrees that the admission is appropriate.[17]

In addition to the rights of minors in relation to their families, attention has been focused on the rights of children in relation to the social and legal systems.[18] One landmark case that sought to protect the rights of minors in regard to the juvenile justice system was *Application of Gault*.[19] Prior to this case, juveniles charged with a crime were not provided the same rights as an adult charged with a crime. The theory behind this difference in practice was that juvenile court was established to protect the best interests of the child, not to treat him as a criminal. However, if a child was found to be delinquent, the consequences could be incarceration for the rest of his minority. *Gault* held that a minor charged with being delinquent was entitled to representation by counsel to a certain other due process rights. The key focus of *Gault* and subsequent decisions was to extend the due process rights afforded adult criminals to juveniles without abolishing the special consideration provided juveniles. This same theory has been applied to proceedings in noncourt settings and to conflicts between parents and children.[20]

Finally, there has been litigation to protect the interests of children in institutions. The cases dealt with abuses and excesses in juvenile detention centers as well as lack of proper care and treatment in institutions such as retardation facilities.[21] Class action lawsuits and individual lawsuits were included. Although there has been no definitive court decision on this issue, it is clear that, with few exceptions, juveniles have the same rights as adults, particularly with regard to the right to treatment. Additionally, a minor has a right to education while institutionalized.

Nursing Implications. When a psychiatric nurse is involved in treating a minor, it is important to determine whether anyone other than the parent has the right to provide consent for treatment. Even if the state law recognizes the right of the minor to consent in certain situations, or even if the minor is emancipated, the parent may still have rights that have to be recognized. Therefore, the issue of consent should always be clarified and documented in the juvenile's record.

References

1. Monroe E. Trout: When Can a Child Consent to Treatment? *Legal Aspects of Medical Practice,* September 1978, pp. 25–28
2. *Tennessee Code Annotated,* 57-5-301(e).
3. Trout: When Can a Child Consent, pp. 25–28.
4. Ibid.
5. Ibid., p. 25.
6. Ralph Reisner: *Law and the Mental Health System,* St. Paul, Minn., West Publishing Co., 1985, p. 188.
7. Ibid.
8. The Uncertain Status of the Emancipated Minor: Why We Need a Uniform Statutory Emancipation of Minors Act (USEMA). *University of San Francisco Law Review,* 15, Spring-Summer 181, pp. 473–507.
9. Ibid., p. 476.
10. Ibid.
11. Ibid., p. 477.
12. Trout: When Can a Child Consent, p. 25.
13. Jane Knitzer: Children's Rights in the Family and Society: Dilemmas and Realities. *American Journal of Orthopsychiatry,* 52, no. 3, July 1982, p. 481–495.
14. Ibid.
15. *Tennessee Code Annotated,* 33-601.
16. *Parham v. J.L. & J.R.,* 442 U.S. 584 (1979).
17. Charles Lidz, Ellen Gross, Alan Meisel and Loren Roth: The Rights of Juveniles in Voluntary Psychiatric Commitments: Some Empirical Observations. *Bulletin of the American Academy of Psychiatry and the Law,* 8, no. 2, 1980, pp. 168–232.
18. Knitzer: Children's Rights, p. 487.
19. *Application of Gault,* 407 P.2d 760 (1965).
20. Knitzer: Children's Rights, p. 487.
21. Ibid., pp. 487–490.

CHAPTER 8

Malpractice Issues

Malpractice suits have greatly increased in number within the last several years, and the nurse working in a psychiatric setting now is more likely to be a defendant in a lawsuit than ever before. An individual who thinks he has been aggrieved by a nurse may bring suit in a state or federal court for monetary damages for alleged negligence. Negligence is a civil matter that comes within the purview of tort law. It is a dispute between two or more citizens or business entities in which one claims that the other breached a duty and caused damage.

Elements of Negligence

Before discussing cases that have been filed against professionals, such as nurses, for psychiatric care, it is important to review the elements of negligence as defined in a malpractice action. Malpractice is based on the public expectation that the performance of a professional or specialist will measure up to the standards of the profession or specialty. A person avowing professional status is held to the degree of skill claimed by that profession. Therefore, the test of fault or breach of duty in malpractice cases is determined not by reference to the traditional "reasonable and prudent man" standard used in ordinary personal injury cases, but by a standard that measures whether there was a departure from customary professional conduct. Thus, the legal standard of care for a nurse is that of a "reasonable and prudent" nurse.

It is the legal responsibility of health caregivers to provide safe care.[1] Each individual who provides health care to an individual or family is personally responsible and liable for his or her own conduct. The professional nurse might also be responsible for other professionals through the supervisory process. When a person files a lawsuit against a professional for malpractice, it must first be established that the professional owed a duty to the patient and, further, that his or her practice fell below a reasonable standard of care. Consequently, a nurse must apply the minimum standard of care in her practice that any other reasonably prudent nurse would apply in the same circumstances.

Whether employed by an agency or another individual, or self-employed in private practice, the nurse has a legal duty to give safe and appropriate care to patients and families for whom they have responsibility. A causal link between the treatment or care provided by the nurse and the injury to the patient must also be established. The courts will look at the circumstances of particular events to determine whether it was foreseeable that the individual would be harmed as a result of the nurse's actions. The last element the plaintiff must prove is that an injury was suffered and damages resulted from the nurse's negligence.[2]

Even if a nurse has provided a high standard of care, defense against a possible malpractice action depends on proper documentation that established procedures have been followed. It is important to document care provided in order to avoid malpractice suits.

Abille v. United States of America

The following is a case illustrating these legal concepts. Manuel Abille was 51 years old and had been taking the drug reserpine for high blood pressure.[3] On April 15, 1977, a physician discontinued his use of this drug because the patient had developed depression, a side effect sometimes associated with reserpine. The patient had no prior history of depression or suicidal tendencies. The patient voluntarily admitted himself to the U.S. Air Force Hospital at Elmendorf Air Force Base in Anchorage, Alaska, on April 26, 1977. The following day, he was seen by one of three psychiatrists on the hospital staff. The doctor noted that Mr. Abille had a flattened affect, suicidal ideation for a duration of three weeks, and sleep disturbances. His diagnosis was depressive neurosis, hypertension, and reactive depression to reserpine.

Patients in this facility were assigned a particular status based on their mental condition. Mr. Abille was given S-1 status, which meant that he was not permitted to leave his psychiatric unit without a staff escort. There were no further notations by a physician in record. On April 27, 1977, the nurse's notes stated that Mr. Abille had slept only three hours the preceding night. The following day it was observed and recorded that he had a brighter affect, and he commented that he wished to go home. On April 29 it was indicated that Mr. Abille had not slept well, was anxious, was less depressed, and was resisting group therapy. He further stated his desire to discuss his problems with the physician. On that day, a psychiatric technician wrote that Mr. Abille was depressed; the technician also expressed concern about his suicidal ideation. There were no further notes in the record.

On April 30 the psychiatric nurses assigned to the ward began permitting Mr. Abille the privileges of S-2 status, which meant that he could leave the unit if escorted by a staff member or another patient who was permitted more freedom. Additionally, he could go unescorted to designated places within the hospital for specific purposes.

The government memorandum that described the privileges of an S-2 patient stated that this level was assigned to individuals who had been in the hospital at least 24 hours, were not considered suicidal, and had not demonstrated behaviors that might indicate that the person would be harmful to himself or others. On this particular day, Mr. Abille was allowed to go to Mass unattended in the building. He returned without incident. He was then permitted to use a razor to shave and to go to breakfast without an escort. After he left the ward, he was found dead on the ground outside. He apparently had leaped to his death from an unsupervised lounge on the seventh floor.

There was no written order by the physician to change Mr. Abille's status from S-1 to S-2. However, there was a change of status written by a nurse *after* Mr. Abille's death in response to a verbal order from the physician on April 29. The physician did not appear at the trial, and the court concluded that his answers to questions at a deposition about the change of status orders were not persuasive. It was concluded that no order had been written before the death occurred. The court stated that the nurses had been acting in good faith,

> but the defendant's nurses were acting below the standard of care when they permitted Abille to leave the ward unescorted while he was classified S-1, his status not having been changed by a physician. Inasmuch as he had been diagnosed to be suicidal, his suicide attempt was a foreseeable risk and must therefore be considered as a proximate result of the negligent act of the nurses.[4]

After Mr. Abille's death, the physician had written that the "symptoms of a suicidal disposition continued to be displayed by Abille and recognized by the staff." At the trial, an expert witness testified that risks vary from high to low in relation to suicidal patients. The concept of least restrictive alternative makes it difficult to assess how much freedom to grant a patient, taking into consideration his suicidal potential. The court concluded that the potential for committing suicide was a matter of judgment. However, the physician's failure to keep ongoing progress notes and the lack of a written order for reclassification did fall below the standard of care. The survivors who brought the suit were awarded monetary damages.

This case clearly illustrates that the nurses employed to care for psychiatric patients in this facility did have a legal duty to Mr. Abille. The care fell below the standard when no written order confirming the change of privilege status was placed in the record. Because he was a suicidal risk, it was foreseeable that, with more freedom to move around, he might commit suicide. It was concluded that these acts were the proximate cause of Mr. Abille's death. Because a fatal injury resulted, damages were awarded to the survivors.

Ray v. Ameri-Care Hospital

In a contrasting decision, another hospital was found to be not liable for a patient's suicide. Mr. Ray was admitted on January 14, 1976, with a diagnosis of paranoid schizophrenia. He seemed to do all right for a few hours after admission, but when a laboratory technician attempted to draw blood for tests, the patient had a physical reaction that necessitated calling his physician. Because of his psychotic symptoms, Mr. Ray was given haloperidol (Haldol), and visits were limited to his immediate family. The night of January 18 Mr. Ray appeared to have a restful night but dozed infrequently. In the early morning hours on January 19, 1976, he was found drowned in the bathtub. The record showed that he had a delusion that he was able to breathe underwater. It had been concluded prior to his death that it would be to his detriment to place him in a small room or to use mechanical restraints because of his paranoid symptoms.

The court concluded that it is not possible to take precautions for every delusion that a mentally ill person might experience, and that the physician did not fall below the standard of care in prescribing treatment for Mr. Ray.[5] It should be noted that each case will be determined by the individual facts. The courts will look to the behavior exhibited by the patient prior to the incident and to the professional's response to the symptomatology exhibited.

Delicata v. Bourlesses

In *Delicata v. Bourlesses*, the plaintiffs appealed a ruling by a medical malpractice tribunal, which had decided that the following facts did "not present a legitimate question of liability appropriate for judicial inquiry."[6] Carmela Delicata was 39 years of age and was suffering from cancer. She had had several surgeries performed, but the cancer had metastasized to her bones. She began receiving chemotherapy.

In November 1975, she attempted suicide in the presence of her daughter. She was subsequently hospitalized in the psychiatric ward of New England Deaconess Hospital on November 17, 1975. On November 19, she expressed thoughts of suicide and asked the staff to "assist in this task of suicide."[7] She was seen by a staff psychiatrist and a psychologist, who both indicated that suicidal precautions and constant supervision were not necessary. However, she continued to be depressed, and on November 22 it was recommended by a staff psychiatrist that she begin electroconvulsive therapy in two days.

She was asked to discuss the therapy with her husband. She apparently did not want the electroconvulsive therapy, and she was overheard by another patient, who subsequently related to the staff that she told her husband she wanted to die. The husband became disgusted with her and left. Mrs. Delicata was last seen at 9:00 p.m., when she went to take a bath. Forty minutes later she was found fully clothed, submerged in a water-filled tub. She was given resuscitation without success.

A nurse expert witness testified that, based on her examination of the patient's records, the patient should have been observed at least every 15 minutes. She further testified that because the patient was not observed for a 40-minute period (which was unacceptable nursing practice), the nurse's negligence contributed to the cause of death.[8] The court subsequently ruled that

> despite the psychiatrist's finding three days before that suicidal precautions were unnecessary, a reasonably skillful nurse in the defendant's position, would at a minimum have monitored Mrs. Delicata during the bath, based on the patient's condition that evening, or should either have instituted closer supervision on her own initiative or sought permission from a staff physician to implement stricter controls.[9]

The court concluded that there was a legitimate question of lability and that further judicial inquiry was indicated. Irene Murchison and associates comment in a book on legal aspects of nursing that "it is a significant legal decision to hold the nurse accountable for failure to use the knowledge and skills of a professional psychiatric nurse in developing and sustaining a plan of care based on continuing reassessment of patient needs."[10] It should be noted that the nurse in this case was sued personally, an occurrence that is becoming more frequent.

Documentation

As these case studies illustrate, an important aspect of care of the mental health client is an adequate documentation of the assessment, diagnosis, and treatment plans and care of the individual. Not only is this documentation necessary as a record of care for the client, but it is also important in communicating with other personnel about the individual's prior and continuing care.

To characterize the client's condition accurately, a descriptive account utilizing the senses should be implemented: what is seen, what is heard, what is smelled, and what is felt (for example, skin temperature). Such accounts should also describe any therapeutic interventions undertaken.[11] Only the facts should be presented; conclusions should be left to the reader. Continuity of care should be recorded in the notes, and any teaching concerning medications and instructions about aftercare plans should be documented. Any reviewer should be able to ascertain that the treatment plan was implemented or, if it was not, the reasons for the changes. Bias and labeling should be avoided, especially if the nurse is irritated with the patient or client. Individuals with major mental illnesses, particularly the chronically mentally ill, can cause professionals to become discouraged and impatient when no change is seen in their behavior. There should be no unsolved mysteries within the record. Only standard abbreviations or abbreviations approved by the health care facility should be in the record. Misspelled words and poor grammar should be avoided. If there is a change in a patient's condition, the person notified and the time of the report should be clearly indicated.

When any question about the record is raised by the client, an attorney, or the courts, the record will probably be subpoenaed and examined. Records are important as an account of client care, and they also will be supportive of the nurse who has provided proper care but is nonetheless named a defendant in a lawsuit. Treatment plans should be supported in the record by noting their implementation. When treatment is not recorded, unless an extraordinary amount of evidence is presented to the contrary, it will probably be considered not to have been done.

The case of *Williams v. United States of America* presents a situation in which information was recorded but not communicated to law officers in the community as requested.[12] Mr. Alonzo Bush was on parole in California when he sustained a severe head injury that necessitated brain surgery. Following this procedure, he was allowed to go to South Dakota by the California Parole Board. He was admitted to the Veterans

Administration (VA) Hospital at Hot Springs, South Dakota, in September 1973. The symptoms listed by the admitting doctor included organic brain syndrome and a psychotic disorder. In the next two and a half years, Mr. Bush was admitted and discharged from VA hospitals 23 times.

In January 1975, while a patient at the VA Hospital in Hot Springs, Mr. Bush attacked another patient without provocation. The parole officer was called, and the sheriff apprehended Mr. Bush at the VA Hospital and incarcerated him. This information was included in the medical record. At the end of January, Mr. Bush transferred to an alcoholic treatment ward in Yankton, South Dakota. He was released from this program in March 1975.

Mr. Bush was later admitted to another VA facility at Fort Meade in Maryland. During this stay he attacked a staff member, wrestling him to the ground. Because he had signed out against advice, he was escorted out of the hospital. He was returned to the hospital the next day, and the staff was instructed to notify the police upon his departure. There was much subsequent discussion among the treatment staff about what to do with Mr. Bush. It was finally decided that he did not meet commitment standards. Mr. Bush left the locked ward of the VA Hospital and was jailed by the sheriff. He attempted to set fire to the jail. Because they could not control him, he was returned to the hospital, again with instructions to contact law enforcement officials on his discharge.

Mr. Bush requested to be transferred from the locked ward to the alcoholic treatment ward. He was subsequently discharged from the program by a physician who had not thoroughly read the record. The law enforcement officials were not notified. Mr. Bush became embroiled in an altercation, pulled a revolver, and shot and killed a man. A surviving relative of the victim filed a lawsuit against the federal government for wrongful death.

The court ruled that the hospital had been requested to notify the police upon Bush's release. This information was contained in the record. There was a failure on the part of the hospital to act responsibly, contributing substantially to the victim's death, and the hospital was found liable for the damages resulting from the wrongful death. This case illustrates the importance of being informed about a patient's history, of the critical issue of aftercare planning for such an individual, and of the necessity for good communication within an institutional system.

In *Pisel v. Stamford Hospital*, the plaintiff, a 23-year-old woman, developed choriomeningitis and a urinary infection and subsequently became psychotic.[13] She was hospitalized for six weeks and then resumed her work. Two months posthospitalization she discontinued treatment with a psychiatrist. The following January she developed psychotic symptoms. She was admitted to Stamford Hospital on January 14, 1976, and medication was ordered on January 21. The order was not recorded until the following day, but the medication was out of stock. The physician was not notified. On January 24, without medication, the patient became very agitated and attempted to leave the unit on three occasions during the morning. She communicated to a staff member that she was hearing voices telling her to injure herself. She had previously responded to voices telling her not to eat or take her medication. No one spoke with or assessed the plaintiff from 6:15 a.m. until 10:00 a.m., although she was seen at 9:50 a.m. After 10:00 a.m. she was found with her head lodged between the side rail and the mattress of her bed. She was unconscious with no pulse, blood pressure, or respiratory function. She was left with residual brain damage and will need care in a skilled nursing home for the remainder of her life. Several days after the incident the director of nursing "ordered" the staff who had provided nursing care to the plaintiff to rewrite the record. The court, in a ruling upholding the lower court which entered a verdict for the plaintiff, ruled:

> The substituted record was demonstrably false and conflicted with other records and the testimony of staff members on duty that morning as to their actual observations. The revised record came to light after suit was commenced when a nurse not connected with the psychiatric unit brought to the attention of the hospital administration that she had been forced to rewrite a note on the original record. The trial court instructed the jury without objection that they could consider the substitution of the records as a circumstance indicating the defendant's consciousness of negligence.[14]

Medical records should never be altered in an attempt to hide negligence. The correct method for correcting an error is to strike through the note and write "error." In this manner, the incorrect writing can also be read and there is no question of an attempt to falsify a record.

The Nurse as a Witness

There are two capacities in which a nurse might be called upon to testify, as a lay witness and as an expert witness at a hearing or trial. In situations in which the nurse is asked to testify as a lay witness, she will testify to the facts and be asked to describe what she observed, any communications to her, or information she might have overheard.[15] These data would come from the nurse's direct knowledge. An accurate recording of patient care and good observational skills will be helpful to a nurse in this situation.

When called on as an expert witness, the nurse is permitted to give opinions. In matters defining the standard of care given by the nurse to psychiatric patients, the witness could be a psychiatric nurse defining the accepted practice. The nurse is an expert when the knowledge she possesses is specialized and when because of nursing experience, expertise, and information she can define standards of practice. Preparation time for this endeavor can be lengthy. However, it is important that nurses provide this service to improve patient care. They also are the best evaluators of nursing care.

In a 1986 case, *Kanter v. Metropolitan Medical Center*, a suit was brought by a trustee for the wrongful death of a 31-year-old woman who died while left in the bathtub by a registered psychiatric nurse.[16] The issue was raised as to whether a psychiatric nurse needed to testify as an expert witness to determine the standard of care. The trustee asserted that giving a patient a bath requires no special knowledge and that the jury did not need to hear an expert. The Court of Appeals of Minnesota upheld the trial court's ruling that an expert witness was needed, stating, "In a psychiatric ward the potential tendencies of patients suffering from mental illness are not so easily determined by one without a special training and knowledge."[17]

Recently, courts and authors have acknowledged that nurses are the experts where nursing care is concerned. W. T. Eccard states in a law review article that "allowing a physician to testify in nursing malpractice actions or a nurse to testify in medical malpractice actions simply because they share common areas of knowledge unnecessarily confuses the issue."[18]

Vicarious Liability

The concept of vicarious liability, or *respondeat superior* ("let the master speak"), is predicated on the employer's relationship with his employees. It is the institution's responsibility to employ stable, knowledgeable people, and an institution can indeed be held liable for the misconduct and negligence of its employees. It is within the institution's purview both to begin and to terminate employment, as is the case with virtually any employer.

This accountability of the institution and its ability to absorb and spread the costs of any financial burden resulting from legal liability have largely precluded legal actions against individual nurses. At one time, too, it was difficult to obtain financial remuneration from nurses sued individually because of the relatively low economic status of the profession. This situation has gradually changed, and lawsuits against individual nurses are being filed in increasing numbers.

Some nurses believe that as long as the employer is answerable for their conduct, they are absolved of individual responsibility. Although it is true that an employer is held accountable for its employees' actions, a nurse is always accountable for professional behavior in relation to client care.

In a landmark case, *Darling v. Charleston Community Memorial Hospital*, a hospital was held liable for not calling in consultants to help a physician care for a young man who had sustained a broken leg.[19] The nurses observed the steadily deteriorating condition of the man's leg and failed to report the situation to the hospital administration.

The court defined a new duty for the nurse, "that of informing the hospital administration of any deviation in proper medical care that poses a threat to the well-being of the patient."[20] According to the bylaws of the hospital and the Standards for Hospital Accreditation promulgated by the Joint Commission on Accreditation of Hospitals, the hospital should have reviewed the work of the physician or required consultation when the patient failed to respond to treatment. It is therefore the duty of the nurse to report to the administration any situation in which a professional doctor or nurse is not administering the acceptable standard of care.

Other Standards of Care

Standards have been developed by the American Nurses' Association and other nursing organizations regarding the delivery of nursing care. The standards established by the association, as well as those set by organizations coordinating Medicare and Medicaid payments, are in many cases higher than the minimum standards traditionally required by the courts. Because these standards are steadily being raised, in the future the courts may use these higher standards to determine liability.

References

1. Mary D. Hemelt and Mary Ellen Mackert: *Dynamics of Law in Nursing and Health Care*, 2nd ed., Reston, Va., Reston Publishing Co., 1982, p. 22.
2. Ibid.
3. *Abille v. United States of America*, 484 F.Supp. 703 (1980).
4. Ibid., p. 707.
5. *Ray v. Ameri-Care Hospital*, 400 So.2d 1127 (1981).
6. *Delicata v. Bourlesses*, 404 N.E.2d 667 (1980), at 668.
7. Ibid., at 669.
8. Ibid., at 670.
9. Ibid., at 671.
10. Irene Murchison, Thomas S. Nichols and Rachel Hanson: *Legal Accountability in the Nursing Process*, 2nd ed., St. Louis, C. V. Mosby Co., 1982, p. 168.
11. Hemelt and Mackert: *Dynamics of Law*, p. 178. See also Alice Kerr: Nurses Notes, That's Where the Goodies Are! *Nursing 75*, February 175, pp. 34–40.
12. *Williams v. United States of America*, 450 F.Supp. 1040 (S.D. 1978).
13. *Pisel v. Stamford Hospital*, 430 A.2d 1 (Conn. 1980).
14. Ibid., at 6.
15. Murchison, Nichols and Hanson: *Legal Accountability*, p. 106.
16. *Kanter v. Metropolitan Medical Center*, 384 N.W.2d 914 (1986).
17. Ibid., at 916.

18. W. T. Eccard: Revolution in White—New Approaches in Treating Nurses as Professionals. *Vanderbilt Law Review*, 30, 1977, p. 865.
19. *Darling v. Charleston Community Memorial Hospital*, 33 Ill.2d 253, 211 N.E.2d 326 (1965).
20. Irene Murchison and Thomas S. Nichols: *Legal Foundations of Nursing Practice*, New York, Macmillan Co., 1970, p. 142.

Changes in mental health law have been numerous and continuous in the 1970s and 1980s. It can be anticipated that changes will continue. Nurses practicing in the mental health field must be cognizant of the laws as they evolve. Attending continuing education programs and reading journals and books can help in keeping up with the changes; however, on specific issues there is no substitute for legal advice and counsel from an attorney, whether retained by the mental health facility where the nurse is employed or individually by the nurse.

It is hoped that the information in this book will stimulate nurses to review their own practices and to question those individuals who might violate patients' rights. Nurses traditionally have been advocates for quality health care but have often felt powerless to make changes because of a lack of knowledge and political power. Since nurses are responsible for their own individual practices, keeping abreast of mental health law will enable the nurse to make informed judgments about practice in order to provide quality care to clients and ensure their rights.

Psychiatric nursing faces challenges in the years ahead. Cutbacks in funding at the federal level because of continuing budget deficits may force states to decrease their support for mental health programs, thus increasing the likelihood that patients' rights will be violated. Vigilance must be maintained so that a reversion back to the days of substandard care for the mentally ill does not occur. Informed nurses attuned to the standards set by our profession, newly passed statutes, and evolving case law can influence the adequate provision of care not only in the institution but in community programs as well.

Title II—Restatement of Bill of Rights for Mental Health Patients (P.L. 99-319)

Restatement of Bill of Rights

Sec. 201. It is the sense of the Congress that, as previously stated in title V of the Mental Health Systems Act, each State should review and revise, if necessary, its laws to ensure that mental health patients receive the protection and services they require, and that in making such review and revision, States should take into account the recommendations of the President's Commission on Mental Health and the following:

(1) A person admitted to a program or facility for the purpose of receiving mental health services should be accorded the following:
  (A) The right to appropriate treatment and related services in a setting and under conditions that –
    (i)   are the most supportive of such person's personal liberty; and
    (ii) restrict such liberty only to the extent necessary consistent with such person's treatment needs, applicable requirements of law, and applicable judicial orders.

(B) The right to an individualized, written, treatment or service plan (such plan to be developed promptly after admission of such person), the right to treatment based on such plan, the right to periodic review and reassessment of treatment and related service needs, and the right to appropriate revision of such plan, including any revision necessary to provide a description of mental health services that may be needed after such person is discharged from such program or facility.

(C) The right to ongoing participation, in a manner appropriate to such person's capabilities, in the planning of mental health services to be provided such person (including the right to participate in the development and periodic revision of the plan described in subparagraph (B), and, in connection with such participation, the right to be provided with reasonable explanation, in terms and language appropriate to such person's condition and ability to understand, of –

   (i)   such person's general mental condition, and, if such program or facility has provided a physical examination, such person's general physical condition;

   (ii)   the objectives of treatment;

   (iii) the nature and significant possible adverse effects of recommended treatments;

   (iv)   the reasons why a particular treatment is considered appropriate;

   (v)   the reasons why access to certain visitors may not be appropriate; and

   (vi)   any appropriate and available alternative treatments, services, and types of providers of mental health services.

(D) The right not to receive a mode or course of treatment, established pursuant to the treatment plan, in the absence of such person's informed, voluntary, written consent to such mode or course of treatment –

    (i)   during an emergency situation if such treatment is pursuant to or documented contemporaneously by the written order of a responsible mental health professional; or

    (ii) as permitted under applicable law in the case of a person committed by a court to a treatment program or facility.

(E) The right not to participate in experimentation in the absence of such person's informed, voluntary, written consent, the right to appropriate protections in connection with such participation, including the right to a reasonable explanation of the procedure to be followed, the benefits to be expected, the relative advantages of alternative treatments, and the potential discomforts and risks, and the right and opportunity to revoke such consent.

(F) The right to freedom from restraint or seclusion, other than as a mode or course of treatment or restraint or seclusion during an emergency situation if such restraint or seclusion is pursuant to or documented contemporaneously by the written order of a responsible mental health professional.

(G) The right to a humane treatment environment that affords reasonable protection from harm and appropriate privacy to such person with regard to personal needs.

(H) The right to confidentiality of such person's records.

(I) The right to access, upon request, to such person's mental health care records, except such person may be refused access to –

    (i)   information in such records provided by a third party under assurance that such information shall remain confidential; and

    (ii) specific material in such records if the health professional responsible for the mental health services concerned has made a determination in writing that such access would be detrimental to such person's health, except that such material may be made available to a similarly licensed health professional selected by such person, and such health professional selected may, in the exercise of professional judgement, provide such person with access to any or all parts of such material or otherwise disclose the information contained in such material to such person.

(J) The right, in the case of a person admitted on a residential or inpatient care basis, to converse with others privately, to have convenient and reasonable access to the telephone and mails, and to see visitors during regularly scheduled hours, except that, if a mental health professional treating such person determines that denial of access to a particular visitor is necessary for treatment purposes, such mental health professional may, for a specific, limited, and reasonable period of time, deny such access if such mental health professional has ordered such denial in writing and such order has been incorporated in the treatment plan for such person. An order denying such access should include the reasons for such denial.

(K) The right to be informed promptly at the time of admission and periodically thereafter, in language and terms appropriate to such person's condition and ability to understand, of the rights described in this section.

(L) The right to assert grievances with respect to infringement of the rights described in this section, including the right to have such grievances considered in a fair, timely, and impartial grievance procedure provided for or by the program or facility.

(M) Notwithstanding subparagraph (J), the right of access to (including the opportunities and facilities for private communication with) any available –

(i)   rights protection service within the program or facility;

(ii) rights protection service within the State mental health system designed to be available to such person;

(iii) system established under title I to protect and advocate the rights of mentally ill individuals; and

(iv) qualified advocate;
      for the purpose of receiving assistance to understand, exercise, and protect the rights described in this section and in other provisions of law.

(N) The right to exercise the rights described in this section without reprisal, including reprisal in the form of denial of any appropriate, available treatment.

(O) The right to referral as appropriate to other providers of mental health services upon discharge.

(2) (A) The rights described in this section should be in addition to and not in derogation of any other statutory or constitutional rights.

(B) The rights to confidentiality of and access to records as provided in subparagraphs (H) and (I) of paragraph (1) should remain applicable to records pertaining to a person after such person's discharge from a program or facility.

(3) (A) No otherwise eligible person should be denied admission to a program or facility for mental health services as a reprisal for the exercise of the rights described in this section.

(B) Nothing in this section should –

(i)   obligate an individual mental health or health professional to administer treatment contrary to such professional's clinical judgment;

(ii) prevent any program or facility from discharging any person for whom the provision of appropriate treatment, consistent with the clinical judgment of the mental health professional primarily responsible for such person's treatment, is or has become impossible as a result of such person's refusal to consent to such treatment;

(iii) require a program or facility to admit any person who, while admitted on prior occasions to such program or facility, has repeatedly frustrated the purposes of such admissions by withholding consent to proposed treatment; or

(iv) obligate a program or facility to provide treatment services to any person who is admitted to such program or facility solely for diagnostic or evaluative purposes.

(C) In order to assist a person admitted to a program or facility in the exercise or protection of such person's rights, such person's attorney or legal representatives should have reasonable access to –

(i)   such person;

(ii) the areas of the program or facility where such person has received treatment, resided, or had access; and

(iii) pursuant to the written authorization of such person, the records and information pertaining to such person's diagnosis, treatment, and related services described in paragraph (1) (I).

(D) Each program and facility should post a notice listing and describing, in language and terms appropriate to the ability of the persons to whom such notice is addressed to understand the rights described in this section of all persons admitted to such program or facility. Each such notice should conform to the format and content for such notices, and should be posted in all appropriate locations.

(4) (A) In the case of a person adjudicated by a court of competent jurisdiction as being incompetent to exercise the

right to consent to treatment or experimentation described in subparagraph (D) or (E) of paragraph (1), or the right to confidentiality of or access to records described in subparagraph (H) or (I) of such paragraph, or to provide authorization as described in paragraph (3) (C) (iii), such right may be exercised or such authorization may be provided by the individual appointed by such court as such person's guardian or representative for the purpose of exercising such right or such authorization.

(B) In the case of a person who lacks capacity to exercise the right to consent to treatment or experimentation under subparagraph (D) or (E) of paragraph (1), or the right to confidentiality of or access to records described in subparagraph (H) or (I) of such paragraph, or to provide authorization as described in paragraph (3)(C)(iii), because such person has not attained an age considered sufficiently advanced under State law to permit the exercise of such right or such authorization to be legally binding, such right may be exercised or such authorization may be provided on behalf of such person by a parent or legal guardian of such person.

(C) Notwithstanding subparagraphs (A) and (B), in the case of a person admitted to a program or facility for the purpose of receiving mental health services, no individual employed by or receiving any remuneration from such program or facility should act as such person's guardian or representative.